TALES OUT OF TIME

Other books edited by Barbara Ireson

FANTASY TALES

HAUNTING TALES

SHADOWS AND SPELLS

THE FABER BOOK OF NURSERY VERSE

THE FABER BOOK OF NURSERY STORIES

By Barbara Ireson

YOUR BOOK OF PARTY GAMES

TALES OUT OF TIME

Edited by

BARBARA IRESON

FABER AND FABER
London · Boston

First published in 1979
by Faber and Faber Ltd.,
3 Queen Square London WC1
Phototypeset in V.I.P. Sabon by
Western Printing Services Ltd, Bristol
Printed in Great Britain by
Redwood Burn Limited, Trowbridge and Esher

British Library Cataloguing
in Publication Data

Tales out of time.
1. Fantastic fiction, English
I. Ireson, Barbara
823'.9'1J PZ5

ISBN 0-571-11410-5

Contents

Acknowledgements

The editor is grateful for permission to use the following copyright material: "Pawley's Peepholes" from *The Seeds of Time* by John Wyndham, published by Michael Joseph.
"Light of Other Days" by Bob Shaw. Copyright © 1966 by The Conde Nast Publications, Inc. Reprinted by permission of the author and the author's agents, Scott Meredith Literary Agency, Inc., 845 Third Avenue, New York, New York 10022, U.S.A.
"Time Has No Boundaries" from *I Love Galesburg in the Springtime* by Jack Finney, published by Eyre & Spottiswoode Ltd. Reprinted by permission of A. D. Peters. © by Jack Finney. Reprinted by permission of Harold Matson Company Inc.
"Alice's Godmother" from *Collected Stories for Children* by Walter de la Mare. Reprinted by permission of the Literary Trustees of Walter de la Mare and the Society of Authors as their representative.
"The Shape of Things" by Ray Bradbury. © 1948 by Ray Bradbury. Reprinted by permission of A. D. Peters & Co., Ltd, and Harold Matson Company Inc.
"Time Travelling" from *The Time Machine* by H. G. Wells, reprinted by permission of the Estate of the late H. G. Wells and the publishers, William Heinemann Ltd.
"Blemish" by John Christopher.
"The Love Letter" by Jack Finney. © 1959 by Jack Finney. Reprinted by permission of Harold Matson Company Inc.

"Hallowe'en for Mr Faulkner" by August Derleth.
"Phantas" from *Widdershins* by Oliver Onions, reprinted by permission of the Estate of the late Oliver Onions.
"The New Accelerator" by H. G. Wells, reprinted by permission of the Estate of the late H. G. Wells.
"Trying to Connect You" by John Rowe Townsend from *The Eleventh Ghost Book* edited by Aidan Chambers, published by Pan Books Ltd.
"A Sound of Thunder" from *Golden Apples of the Sun* by Ray Bradbury. © 1952 by Ray Bradbury. Reprinted by permission of Harold Matson Company Inc.
"Deadline" from *Shock II* by Richard Matheson, reprinted by permission of A. D. Peters & Co., Ltd. © 1964 by Richard Matheson, reprinted by permission of Harold Matson Company Inc.

Pawley's Peepholes

JOHN WYNDHAM

When I called round at Sally's I showed her the paragraph in the *Westwich Evening News*.

"What do you think of that?" I asked her.

She read it, standing, and with an impatient frown on her pretty face.

"I don't believe it," she said, finally.

Sally's principles of belief and disbelief are a thing I've never got quite lined up. How a girl can dismiss a pack of solid evidence as though it were kettle steam, and then go and fall for some advertisement that's phoney from the first word as though it were holy writ, I just don't . . . Oh, well, it keeps on happening, anyway.

This paragraph read:

MUSIC WITH A KICK

Patrons of the concert at the Adams Hall last night were astonished to see a pair of legs dangling knee-deep from the ceiling during one of the items. The whole audience saw them, and all reports agree that they were bare legs, with some kind of sandals on the feet. They remained visible for some three or four minutes, during which time they several times moved back and forth across the ceiling. Finally, after making a kicking movement, they disappeared upwards, and were seen no more. Examination of the roof shows no traces, and the owners of the Hall are at a loss to account for the phenomenon.

"It's just one more thing," I said.

"What does it prove, anyway?" said Sally, apparently forgetful that she was not believing it.

"I don't know that – yet," I admitted.

"Well, there you are, then," she said.

Sometimes I get the feeling that Sally has no real respect for logic.

However, most people were thinking the way Sally was, more or less, because most people like things to stay nice and normal. But it had already begun to look to me as if there were things happening that ought to be added together and make something.

The first man to bump up against it – the first I can find on record, that is – was one Constable Walsh. It may be that others before him saw things, and just put them down as a new kind of pink elephant; but Constable Walsh's idea of a top-notch celebration was a mug of strong tea with a lot of sugar, so when he came across a head sitting up on the pavement on what there was of its neck, he stopped to look at it pretty hard. The thing that really upset him, according to the report he turned in when he had run half a mile back to the station and stopped gibbering, was that it had looked back at him.

Well, it isn't good to find a head on a pavement at any time, and 2 a.m. does somehow make it worse, but as for the rest, well, you can get what looks like a reproachful glance from a cod on a slab if your mind happens to be on something else. Constable Walsh did not stop there, however. *He* reported that the thing opened its mouth "as if it was trying to say something". If it did, he should not have mentioned it; it just naturally brought the pink elephants to mind. However, he stuck to it, so after they had examined him and taken disappointing sniffs at his breath, they sent him back with another man to show just where he had found the thing. Of course, there wasn't any head, nor blood, nor signs of cleaning up. And that's about all there was to the incident – save, doubtless, a few curt remarks on a conduct-sheet to dog Constable Walsh's future career.

But the Constable hadn't a big lead. Two evenings later a block of flats was curdled by searing shrieks from a Mrs Rourke in No. 35, and simultaneously from a Miss Farrell who lived above her. When the neighbours arrived, Mrs Rourke was hysterical about a pair of legs that had been dangling from her bedroom ceiling, and Miss Farrell the same about an arm and shoulder that had stretched out from under her bed. But there was nothing to be seen on the ceiling, and nothing more than a discreditable amount of dust to be found under Miss Farrell's bed.

And there were a number of other incidents, too.

It was Jimmy Lindlen who works, if that isn't too strong a word for it, in the office next to mine who drew my attention to them in the first place. Jimmy collects facts. His definition of a fact is anything that gets printed in a newspaper – poor fellow. He doesn't mind a lot what subjects his facts cover as long as they look queer. I suspect that he once heard that the truth is never simple, and deduced from that that everything that's not simple must be true.

I was used to him coming into my room, full of inspiration, and didn't take much account of it, so when he brought in his first batch of cuttings about Constable Walsh and the rest I didn't ignite much.

But a few days later he was back with some more. I was a bit surprised by his playing the same kind of phenomena twice running, so I gave it a little more attention than usual.

"You see. Arms, heads, legs, torsos, all over the place. It's an epidemic. There's something behind it. *Something's happening!*" he said, as near as one can vocalise italics.

When I had read a few of them I had to admit that this time he had got hold of something where the vein of queerness was pretty constant.

A bus driver had seen the upper half of a body set up vertically in the road before him – but a bit too late. When he stopped and climbed out, sweating, to examine the mess, there was nothing there. A woman hanging out of a window, watching the street, saw another head below her doing the same, but this one was projecting out of the solid brickwork. Then there was a pair of arms that had risen out of the floor of a butcher's shop and seemed to grope for something; after a minute or two they had withdrawn into the solid cement without trace – unless one were to count some detriment to the butcher's trade. There was the man on a building job who had become aware of a strangely dressed figure standing close to him, but supported by empty air – after which he had to be helped down and sent home. Another figure was noticed between the rails in the path of a heavy goods train, but was found to have vanished without trace when the train had passed.

While I skimmed through these and some others, Jimmy stood waiting, like a soda siphon. I didn't have to say more than, "Huh!"

"You see," he said. "Something *is* happening."

"Supposing it is," I conceded cautiously, "then what is it?"

"The manifestation zone is limited," Jimmy told me impressively, and produced a town plan. "If you look where I've marked the incidents you'll see that they're grouped. Somewhere in that circle is 'the focus of disturbance'." This time he managed to vocalise the inverted commas, and waited for me to register amazement.

"So?" I said. "Disturbance of just what?"

He dodged that one.

"I've a pretty good idea now of the cause," he told me weightily.

That was normal, though it might be a different idea an hour later.

"I'll buy it," I offered.

"Teleportation!" he announced. "That's what it is. Bound to come sooner or later. Now someone's on to it."

"H'm," I said.

"But it *must* be." He leaned forward earnestly. "How else'd you account for it?"

"Well, if there could be teleportation, or teleportage, or whatever it is, surely there would have to be a transmitter and some sort of reassembly station," I pointed out. "You couldn't expect a person or object to be kind of broadcast and then come together again in any old place."

"But you don't *know* that," he said. "Besides, that's part of what I was meaning by 'focus'. The transmitter is somewhere else, but focused on that area."

"If it is," I said, "he seems to have got his levels and positions all to hell. I wonder just what happens to a fellow who gets himself reassembled half in and half out of a brick wall?"

It's details like that that get Jimmy impatient.

"Obviously it's early stages. Experimental," he said.

It still seemed to me uncomfortable for the subject, early stages or not, but I didn't press it.

That evening was the first time I mentioned it to Sally, and, on the whole, it was a mistake. After making it quite clear that she didn't believe it, she went on to say that if it was true it was probably just another invention.

"What do you mean, 'just another invention'? Why, it'd be revolutionary!" I told her.

"The wrong kind of revolution, the way we'd use it."

"Meaning?" I asked.

Sally was in one of her withering moods. She turned on her disillusioned voice.

"We've got two ways of using inventions," she said. "One is to kill more people more easily: the other is to enable quick-turnover spivs to make easy money out of suckers. Maybe there are a few exceptions like X-rays, but not many. Inventions! What we do with the product of genius is first of all ram it down to the lowest common denominator and then multiply it by the vulgarest possible fraction. What a century! What a world! When I think what other centuries are going to say about ours it makes me go hot all over."

"I shouldn't worry. You won't be hearing them," I said.

The withering eye was on me.

"I should have known. That is a remark well up to the Twentieth-Century standard."

"You're a funny girl," I told her. "I mean, the way you think may be crazy, but you do do it, in your own way. Now most girls' futures are all cloud-cuckoo beyond next season's hat or next year's baby. Outside of that it might be going to snow split atoms for all they care – they've got a comforting feeling deep down that nothing's ever changed much, or ever will."

"A lot you know about what most girls think," said Sally.

"That's what I was meaning. How could I?" I said.

She seemed to have set her mind so firmly against the whole business that I dropped it for the evening.

A couple of days later Jimmy looked into my room again. "He's laid off," he said.

"Who's laid off what?"

"This teleporting fellow. Not a report later than Tuesday. Maybe he knows somebody's on to him."

"Meaning you?" I asked.

"Maybe."

"Well, are you?"

He frowned. "I've started. I took the bearings on the map of all the incidents, and the fix came on All Saints' Church. I had a look all over the place, but I didn't find anything. Still, I must be close – why else'd he stop?"

I couldn't tell him that. Nor could anyone else. But that very evening there was a paragraph about an arm and a leg that some woman had watched travel along her kitchen wall. I showed it to Sally.

"I expect it will turn out to be some new kind of advertisement," she said.

"A kind of secret advertising?" I suggested. Then, seeing the withering look working up again: "How about going to a picture?" I suggested.

It was overcast when we went in; when we came out it was raining hard. Seeing that there was less than a mile to her place, and all the taxis in the town were apparently busy, we decided to walk it. Sally pulled on the hood of her mackintosh, put her arm through mine, and we set out through the rain. For a bit we didn't talk, then:

"Darling," I said, "I know that I can be regarded as a frivolous person with low ethical standards, but has it ever occurred to you what a field there is there for reform?"

"Yes," she said, decisively, but not in the right tone.

"What I mean is," I told her patiently, "if you happened to be looking for a good work to devote your life to, what could be better than a reclamation job on such a character. The scope is tremendous, just— "

"Is this a proposal of some kind?" Sally inquired.

"*Some* kind! I'd have you know – Good God!" I broke off.

We were in Tyler Street. A short street, rainswept now, and empty, except for ouselves. What stopped me was the sudden appearance of some kind of vehicle, further along. I couldn't make it out very clearly on account of the rain, but I had the impression of a small, low-built lorry with several figures in light clothes on it driving across Tyler Street quite quickly, and vanishing. That wouldn't have been so bad if there were any street crossing Tyler Street, but there isn't; it had just come out of one side and gone into the other.

"Did you see what I saw?" I asked.

"But how on earth— ?" she began.

We walked a little further until we came to the place where the thing had crossed, and looked at the solid brick wall on one side and the housefronts on the other.

"You must have been mistaken," said Sally.

"Well, for – *I* must have been mistaken!"

"But it just couldn't have happened, could it?"

"Now, listen, darling—" I began.

But at that moment a girl stepped out from the solid brick about ten feet ahead of us. We stopped, and gaped at her.

I don't know whether her hair would be her own, art and science together can do so much for a girl, but the way she was wearing it, it was like a great golden chrysanthemum a good foot and a half across, and with a red flower set in it a little left of centre. It looked sort of top-heavy. She was wearing some kind of brief pink tunic, silk perhaps, and more appropriate to one of those elderly gentleman floor-shows than Tyler Street on a filthy wet night. What made it a real shocker was the things that had been achieved by embroidery. I never would have believed that any girl could – oh, well, anyway, there she stood, and there we stood. . . .

When I say "she stood", she certainly did, but somehow she did it about six inches above ground level. She looked at us both, then she stared back at Sally just as hard as Sally was staring at her. It must have been some seconds before any of us moved. The girl opened her mouth as if she were speaking, but no sound came. Then she shook her head, made a forget-it gesture, and turned and walked back into the wall.

Sally didn't move. With the rain shining on her mackintosh she looked like a black statue. When she turned so that I could see her face under the hood it had an expression I had never seen there before. I put my arm round her, and found that she was trembling.

"I'm scared, Jerry," she said.

"No need for that, Sal. There's bound to be a simple explanation of some kind," I said, falsely.

"But it's more than that, Jerry. Didn't you see her ? She was exactly like me!"

"She was pretty much like—" I conceded.

"Jerry, she was *exactly* like – I'm – I'm scared."

"Must have been some trick of the light. Anyway, she's gone now," I said.

All the same, Sally was right. That girl was the image of herself. I've wondered about that quite a bit since . . .

Jimmy brought a copy of the morning paper into my room next day. It carried a brief, facetious leader on the number of local citizens who had been seeing things lately.

"They're beginning to take notice, at last," he proclaimed.

"How's your own line going?" I asked.

He frowned. "I'm afraid it can't be quite the way I thought. I reckon it *is* still in the experimental stage, all right, but the transmitter may not be in these parts at all. It could be that this is just the area he has trained it on for tests."

"But why here?"

"How would I know? It has to be somewhere – and the transmitter itself could be anywhere." He paused, struck by a portentous thought. "It might be really serious. Suppose the Russians had a transmitter which could project people – bombs – here by teleportation . . . ?"

"Why here?" I said again. "I should have thought that Harwell or a Royal Arsenal—"

"Experimental, so far," he reminded me.

"Oh," I said, abashed. I went on to tell him what Sally and I had seen the previous night. "She sort of didn't look much like the way I think of Russians," I added.

Jimmy shook his head. "Might be camouflage. After all, behind that curtain they have to get their idea of the way our girls look mostly from magazines and picture papers," he pointed out.

The next day, after about seventy-five per cent of its readers had written in to tell about the funny things they had been seeing, the *News* dropped the facetious angle. In two days more, the thing had become factional, dividing sharply into what you might call the Classical and Modern camps. In the latter, schismatic groups argued the claims of teleportage against three-dimensional projection, or some theory of spontaneous molecular assembly; in the former, opinions could be sorted as beliefs in a ghostly invasion, a suddenly acquired visibility of habitually wandering spirits, or the imminence of Judgement Day. In the heat of debate it was rapidly becoming difficult to tell who had seen how much of what, and who was enthusiastically bent on improving his case at some expense of fact.

On Saturday Sally and I met for lunch. Afterwards, we started off in the car for a little place in the hills which seemed to me an ideal spot for a proposal. But at the main crossing in the High Street the man in front jumped on his brakes. So did I, and the man behind me. The one behind him didn't quite. There was an interesting crunch of metal going on on the other side of the crossing, too. I stood up to see what it was all about, and then pulled Sally up beside me.

"Here we go again," I said. "Look!"

Slap in the middle of the crossing was – well, you could scarcely call it a vehicle – it was more like a flat trolley or platform, about a foot off the ground. And when I say off the ground, I mean just that. No wheels, or legs. It kind of hung there, from nothing. Standing on it, dressed in coloured things like long shirts or smocks, were half a dozen men looking interestedly around them. Along the edge of the platform was lettered: PAWLEY'S PEEPHOLES. One of the men was pointing out All Saints' Church to another; the rest were paying more attention to the cars and the people. The policeman on duty was hanging a goggling face over the edge of his traffic-control box. Then he pulled himself together. He shouted, he blew his whistle, then he shouted again. The men on the platform took no notice at all. The policeman got out of his box and went across the road looking like a volcano that had seen a nice place to erupt.

"Hey!" he shouted to them.

It didn't worry them, but when he got within a yard or two of them they noticed him, and they nudged one another, and grinned. The policeman's face was purplish, he spoke to them luridly, but they just went on watching him with amused interest. He reached a truncheon out of his back pocket, and went closer. He grabbed at a fellow in a yellow shirt – and his arm went right through him.

The policeman stepped back. You could see his nostrils sort of spread, the way a horse's do. Then he took a firmer hold of his truncheon and made a fine circular sweep at the lot of them. They kept on grinning back at him as the stick went through them.

I take off my hat to that policeman. He didn't run. He stared at them for a moment with a very queer expression on his face, then he turned, and walked deliberately back to his box; just as deliberately he signalled the north–south traffic across. The man ahead of me was ready for it. He drove right at, and through, the platform. It began to move, but I'd have nicked it myself, had it been nickable. Sally, looking back, said that it slid away on a curve and disappeared through the front of the Penny Savings Bank.

When we got to the spot I'd had in mind the weather had come over bad to make the place look dreary and unpropitious, so we drove about a bit, and then back to a nice quiet roadside restaurant just outside Westwich. I was getting the conversation round to the mood where I wanted it when who should come across to our table but Jimmy.

"Fancy meeting you two!" he said. "Did you hear what happened at the Crossing this afternoon, Jerry?"

"We were there," I told him.

"You know, Jerry, this is something bigger than we thought – a whole lot bigger. That platform thing. These people are away ahead of us technically. Do you know what I reckon they are?"

"Martians?" I suggested.

He stared at me, taken aback. "Now, how on earth did *you* guess that?" he said, amazedly.

"I sort of saw it had to come," I admitted. "But," I added, "I do have a kind of feeling that Martians wouldn't be labelled 'Pawley's Peepholes'."

"Oh, were they? Nobody told me that," said Jimmy.

He went away sadly, but even by breaking in at all he had wrecked the mood I'd been building up.

On Monday morning our typist, Anna, arrived even more scatterated than commonly.

"The most terrible thing happened to me," she told us as soon as she was inside the door. "Oh, dear. And did I blush all over!"

"*All* over?" inquired Jimmy interestedly.

She scorned him.

"There I was in my bath, and when I happened to look up

there was a man in a green shirt, standing watching me. Of course, I screamed, at once."

"Of course," agreed Jimmy. "Very proper. And what happened then, or shouldn't we—"

"He just stood there," said Anna. "Then he sniggered, and walked away *through the wall.* Was I mortified!"

"Very mortifying thing, a snigger," Jimmy agreed.

Anna explained that it was not entirely the snigger that had mortified her. "What I mean is," she said. "Things like that oughtn't to be allowed. If a man is going to be able to walk through a girl's bathroom wall, where is he going to stop?"

Which seemed a pretty fair question.

The boss arrived just then. I followed him into his room. He wasn't looking happy.

"What the hell's going on in this damned town, Jerry?" he demanded. "Wife comes home yesterday. Finds two incredible girls in the sitting-room. Thinks it's something to do with me. First bust-up in twenty years. In the middle of it girls vanish," he said succinctly.

One couldn't do more than make a few sympathetic sounds.

That evening when I went to see Sally I found her sitting on the steps of the house, in the drizzle.

"What on earth— ?" I began.

She gave me a bleak look.

"Two of them came into my room. A man and a girl. They wouldn't go. They just laughed at me. Then they started to behave just as though I weren't there. It got – well, I just couldn't stay, Jerry."

She went on looking miserable, and then suddenly burst into tears.

From then on it was stepped up. There was a brisk, if one-sided, engagement in the High Street next morning. Miss Dotherby, who comes of one of Westwich's most respected families, was outraged in every lifelong principle by the appearance of four mop-headed girls who stood giggling on the corner of Northgate. Once she had retracted her eyes and got her breath back, she knew her duty. She gripped her umbrella as if it had been her grandfather's sword, and advanced. She sailed through them, smiting right and left – and when she turned round they were laughing at her. She swiped wildly through them again, and they kept on laughing. Then she started babbling, so someone called an ambulance to take her away.

By the end of the day the town was full of mothers crying shame and men looking staggered, and the Town Clerk and the police were snowed under with demands for somebody to do something about it.

The trouble seemed to come thickest in the district that Jimmy had originally marked out. You *could* meet them elsewhere, but in that area you couldn't help encountering gangs of them, the men in coloured shirts, the girls with their amazing hair-do's and even more amazing decorations on their shirts, sauntering arm-in-arm out of walls, and wandering indifferently through cars and people alike. They'd pause anywhere to point things out to one another and go off into helpless roars of silent laughter. What tickled them most was when people got angry with them. They'd make signs and faces at the stuffier sort until they got them tearing mad – and the madder, the funnier. They ambled as the spirit took them, through shops and banks, and offices, and homes, without a care for the raging occupants. Everybody started putting up "Keep Out" signs; that amused them a lot, too.

It didn't seem as if you could be free of them anywhere in the central area, though they appeared to be operating on levels that weren't always the same as ours. In some places they did have the look of walking on the ground or floor, but elsewhere they'd be inches above it, and then in some places you would encounter them moving along as though they were wading through the solid surface. It was very soon clear that they could no more hear us than we could hear them, so that there was no use appealing to them or threatening them in that way, and none of the notices that people put up seemed to do anything but whet their curiosity.

After three days of it there was chaos. In the worst affected parts there just wasn't any privacy any more. At the most intimate moments they were liable to wander through, visibly sniggering or guffawing. It was all very well for the police to announce that there was no danger, that the visitants appeared unable actually to *do* anything, so the best way was to ignore them. There are times and places when giggling bunches of youths and maidens demand more ignore-power than the average person has got. It could send even a placid fellow like me wild at times, while the women's leagues of this-and-that, and the watch-committee-minded were living in a constant state of blown tops.

The news had begun to get about, and that didn't help, either. News collectors of all kinds came streaming in. They overflowed the place. The streets were snaked with leads to movie cameras, television cameras, and microphones, while the press-photographers were having the snappy-picture time of their lives, and, being solid, they were almost as much of a nuisance as the visitants themselves.

But we hadn't reached the peak of it yet. Jimmy and I happened to be present at the inception of the next stage. We were on our way to lunch, doing our best to ignore visitants, as instructed, by walking through them. Jimmy was subdued. He had had to give up theories because the facts had largely submerged him. Just short of the café we noticed that there was some commotion further up the High Street, and seemingly it was coming our way, so we waited for it. After a bit it emerged through a tangle of halted cars further down, and approached at a rate of some six or seven miles an hour. Essentially it was a platform like the one that Sally and I had seen at the crossroads the previous Saturday, but this was a de luxe model. There were sides to it, glistening with new paint, red, yellow, and blue, enclosing seats set four abreast. Most of the passengers were young, though there was a sprinkling of middle-aged men and women dressed in a soberer version of the same fashions. Behind the first platform followed half a dozen others. We read the lettering on their sides and backs as they went by:

Pawley's Peepholes on the Past – Greatest Invention of the age
History Without Tears – for £1
See How Great Great Grandma Lived
Ye Quainte Olde 20th Century Expresse
See Living History in Comfort – Quaint Dresses, Old Customs
Educational! Learn Primitive Folkways – Living Conditions
Visit Romantic 20th Century – Safety Guaranteed
Know Your History – Get Culture – £1 Trip
Big Money Prize if you Identify Own Granddad/Ma

Most of the people on the vehicles were turning their heads this way and that in gog-eyed wonder interspersed with spasms of giggles. Some of the young men waved their arms at us and produced silent witticisms which sent their companions into inaudible shrieks of laughter. Others leant back comfortably, bit into large, yellow fruits, and munched. They cast occasional glances at the scene, but reserved most of their attention for the ladies whose waists they clasped. On the back of the next-to-last car we read:

Was Great Grandma as Good as she Made Out?
See the Things Your Family History Never Told You

and on the final one:

Spot the Famous before they got Careful – The Real Inside Dope may win you a Big Prize!

As the procession moved away, it left the rest of us looking at one another kind of stunned. Nobody seemed to have much left to say just then.

The show must have been something in the nature of a grand premiere, I fancy, for after that you were liable anywhere in the town to come across a platform labelled something like:

History is Culture – Broaden Your Mind Today
for only £1!

or:

Know the Answers About Your Ancestors

with full, good-time loads aboard, but I never heard of another regular procession.

In the Council Offices they were tearing what was left of their hair, and putting up notices left, right, and centre about what was not allowed to the "tourists" – and giving them more good laughs – but all the while the thing got more embarrassing. Those "tourists" who were on foot took to coming close up and peering into your face, and comparing it with some book or piece of paper they were carrying – after which they looked disappointed and annoyed with you, and moved on to someone else. I came to the conclusion there was no prize at all for finding me.

Well, work has to go on: we couldn't think of any way of dealing with it, so we had to put up with it. Quite a number of families moved out of the town for privacy and to stop their daughters from catching the new ideas about dress, and so on, but most of us just had to keep along as best we could. Pretty nearly everyone one met those days looked either dazed or scowling – except, of course, the "tourists".

I called for Sally one evening about a fortnight after the platform procession. When we came out of the house there was a ding-dong going on further down the road. A couple of girls with heads that looked like globes of gilded basketwork were scratching the daylights out of one another. One of the fellows standing by was looking proud of himself, the rest of the party was whooping things on. We went the other way.

"It just isn't like our town any more," said Sally. "Even our homes aren't ours any more. Why can't they all go away and leave us in peace? Oh, damn them, all of them! I hate them!"

But just outside the park we came upon one little chrysanthemum-head sitting on apparently nothing at all, and crying her heart out. Sally softened a little.

"Perhaps they are human, some of them. But what right have they to turn our town into a horrible fun-fair?"

We found a bench and sat on it, looking at the sunset. I wanted to get her away out of the place.

"It'd be grand away in the hills now," I said.

"It'd be lovely to be there, Jerry," she sighed.

I took her hand, and she didn't pull it away.

"Sally, darling—" I began.

And then, before I could get any further, two tourists, a man and a girl, had to come along and anchor themselves in front of us. That time I was angry. You might see the platforms almost anywhere, but you did reckon to be free of the walking tourists in the park where there was nothing to interest them, anyway – or should not have been. These two, however, had found something. It was Sally, and they stood staring at her, unabashed. She took her hand out of mine. They conferred. The man opened a folder he was carrying, and took a piece of paper out of it. They looked at the paper, then at Sally, then back to the paper. It was too much to ignore. I got up and walked through them to see what the paper was. There I had a surprise. It was a piece of the *Westwich Evening News*, obviously taken from a very ancient copy indeed. It was badly browned and tattered, and to keep it from falling to bits entirely it had been mounted inside some thin, transparent plastic. I wish I had noticed the date, but naturally enough I looked where they were looking – and Sally's face looked back at me from a smiling photograph. She had her arms spread wide, and a baby in the crook of each. I had just time to see the headline: "Twins for Town Councillor's Wife", when they folded up the paper, and made off along the path, running. I reckoned they would be hot on the trail of one of their damned prizes – and I hoped it would turn round and bite them.

I went back and sat down again beside Sally. That picture certainly had spoilt things – "Councillor's Wife"! Naturally she wanted to know what I'd seen on the paper, and I had to sharpen up a few lies to cut my way out of that one.

We sat on awhile, feeling gloomy, saying nothing.

A platform went by, labelled:

Trouble-free Culture – Get Educated in Modern Comfort

We watched it glide away through the railings and into the traffic.

"Maybe it's time we moved," I suggested.

"Yes," agreed Sally, dully.

We walked back towards her place, me still wishing that I had been able to see the date on that paper.

"You wouldn't," I asked her casually, "you wouldn't happen to know any Councillors?"

She looked surprised.

"Well – there's Mr Falmer," she said, rather doubtfully.

"He'd be a – a youngish man?" I inquired, off-handedly.

"Why, no. He's ever so old – as a matter of fact, it's really his wife I know."

"Ah!" I said. "You don't know any of the younger ones?"

"I'm afraid not. Why?"

I put over a line about a situation like this needing young men of ideas.

"Young men of ideas don't have to be councillors," she remarked, looking at me.

Maybe, as I said, she doesn't go much on logic, but she has her own ways of making a fellow feel better. I'd have felt better still if I had had some ideas, though.

The next day found public indignation right up the scale again. It seems there had been an evening service going on in All

Saints' Church. The vicar had ascended his pulpit and was just drawing breath for a brief sermon when a platform labelled:

Was Gt Gt Granddad one of the Boys? – Our £1 Trip may Show you

floated in through the north wall and slid to a stop in front of the lectern. The vicar stared at it for some seconds in silence, then he crashed his fist down on his reading desk.

"This," he boomed. "This is *intolerable*! We shall wait until this *object* is removed."

He remained motionless, glaring at it. The congregation glared with him.

The tourists on the platform had an air of waiting for the show to begin. When nothing happened they started passing round bottles and fruit to while away the time. The vicar maintained his stony glare. When still nothing happened the tourists began to get bored. The young men tickled the girls, and the girls giggled them on. Several of them began to urge the man at the front end of their craft. After a bit he nodded, and the platform slid away through the south wall.

It was the first point our side had ever scored. The vicar mopped his brow, cleared his throat, and then extemporised the address of his life, on the subject of "The Cities of the Plain".

But no matter how influential the tops that were blowing, there was still nothing getting done about it. There were schemes, of course. Jimmy had one of them: it concerned either ultra-high or infra-low frequencies that were going to shudder the projections of the tourists to bits. Perhaps something along those lines might have been worked out sometime, but it was a quicker kind of cure that we were needing; and it is damned difficult to know what you can do about something which is virtually no more than a three-dimensional movie portrait unless you can think up some way of fouling its transmission. All its functions are going on not where you see it, but in some unknown place where the origin is – so how do you get at it? What you are actually seeing doesn't feel, doesn't eat, doesn't breathe, doesn't sleep. . . . It was while I was considering what it actually does do that I had my idea. It struck me all of a heap – so simple. I grabbed my hat and took off for the Town Hall.

By this time the daily processions of sizzling citizens, threateners, and cranks had made them pretty cautious about callers there, but I worked through at last to a man who got interested, though doubtful.

"No one's going to like that much," he said.

"No one's meant to like it. But it couldn't be much worse than this – *and* it's likely to do local trade a bit of good, too," I pointed out.

He brightened a bit at that. I pressed on:

"After all, the Mayor has his restaurants, and the pubs'll be all for it, too."

"You've got a point there," he admitted. "Very well, we'll put it to them. Come along."

For the whole of three days we worked hard on it. On the fourth we went into action. Soon after daylight there were gangs out on all the roads fixing barriers at the municipal limits, and when they'd done that they put up big white boards lettered in red:

WESTWICH
THE CITY THAT LOOKS AHEAD
COME AND SEE
IT'S BEYOND THE MINUTE – NEWER THAN
TOMORROW
SEE
THE WONDER CITY OF THE AGE
TOLL (Non-Residents) 25p

The same morning the television permission was revoked, and the national papers carried large display advertisements:

COLOSSAL! – UNIQUE! – EDUCATIONAL!

WESTWICH
presents the only authentic
FUTURAMATIC SPECTACLE

WANT TO KNOW:
What Your Great Great Granddaughter will Wear?
How Your Great Great Grandson will Look?
Next Century's Styles?
How Customs will Change?

COME TO WESTWICH AND SEE FOR YOURSELF
THE OFFER OF THE AGES
THE FUTURE FOR 25p

We reckoned that with the publicity there had been already there'd be no need for more detail than that – though we ran some more specialised advertisements in the picture dailies:

WESTWICH
GIRLS! GIRLS!! GIRLS!!!
THE SHAPES TO COME
SAUCY FASHIONS – CUTE WAYS
ASTONISHING – AUTHENTIC – UNCENSORED
GLAMOUR GALORE FOR 25p

and so on. We bought enough space to get it mentioned in the news columns in order to help those who like to think they are doing things for sociological, psychological, and other intellectual reasons.

And they came.

There had been quite a few looking in to see the sights before, but now they learnt that it was something worth charging money for the figures jumped right up – and the more they went up, the gloomier the Council Treasurer got because we hadn't made it fifty pence, or even a pound.

After a couple of days we had to take over all vacant lots, and some fields further out, for car parks, and people were parking far enough out to need a special bus service to bring them in. The streets became so full of crowds stooging around greeting any of Pawley's platforms or tourists with whistles, jeers, and catcalls, that local citizens simply stayed indoors and did their smouldering there.

The Treasurer began to worry now over whether we'd be liable for Entertainment Tax. The list of protests to the Mayor grew longer each day, but he was so busy arranging special convoys of food and beer for his restaurants that he had little time to worry about them. Nevertheless, after a few days of it I started to wonder whether Pawley wasn't going to see us out, after all. The tourists didn't care for it much, one could see, and it must have interfered a lot with their prize-hunts, but it hadn't cured them of wandering about all over the place, and now we had the addition of thousands af trippers whooping it up with pandemonium for most of the night. Tempers all round were getting short enough for real trouble to break out.

Then, on the sixth night, when several of us were just beginning to wonder whether it might not be wiser to clear out of Westwich for a bit, the first crack showed – a man at the Town Hall rang me up to say he had seen several platforms with empty seats on them.

The next night I went down to one of their regular routes to see for myself. I found a large, well-lubricated crowd already there, exchanging cracks and jostling and shoving, but we hadn't long to wait. A platform slid out on a slant through the front of the Coronation Café, and the label on it read:

CHARM & ROMANCE OF 20TH CENTURY – 75p

and there were half a dozen empty seats, at that.

The arrival of the platform brought a well-supported Bronx cheer, and a shrilling of whistles. The driver remained indifferent as he steered straight through the crowds. His passengers looked less certain of themselves. Some of them did their best to play up; they giggled, made motions of returning slap for slap and grimace for grimace with the crowd to start with. Possibly it was as well that the tourist girls couldn't hear the things the crowd was shouting to them, but some of the gestures were clear enough. It couldn't have been a lot of fun gliding straight into the men who were making them. By the time the platform was clear of the crowd and disappearing through the front of the Bon Marché pretty well all the tourists had given up pretending that it was; some of them were looking a little sick. By the expression on several of the faces I reckoned that Pawley might be going to have a tough time explaining the culture aspect of it to a deputation somewhere.

The next night there were more empty seats than full ones, and someone reported that the price had come down to fifty pence.

The night after that they did not show up at all, and we all had a busy time with the job of returning the money and refusing claims for wasted petrol.

And the next night they didn't come, either; or the one after that; so then all we had to do was to pitch into the job of cleaning up Westwich, and the affair was practically over – apart from the longer term business of living down the reputation the place had been getting lately.

At least, we say it's over. Jimmy, however, maintains that that is probably only the way it looks from here. According to him, all they had to do was to modify out the visibility factor that was causing the trouble, so it's possible that they are still touring around here – and other places.

Well, I suppose he could be right. Perhaps that fellow Pawley, whoever he is, or will be, has a chain of his funfairs operating all round the world and all through history at this very moment. But we don't know – and, as long as he keeps them out of sight, I don't know that we care a lot, either.

Pawley has been dealt with as far as we are concerned. He was a case for desperate measures; even the vicar of All Saints' appreciated that; and undoubtedly he had a point to make when he began his address of thanksgiving with: "Paradoxical, my friends, paradoxical can be the workings of vulgarity . . . "

Once it was settled I was able to make time to go round and see Sally again. I found her looking brighter than she'd been for weeks, and lovelier on account of it. She seemed pleased to see me, too.

"Hullo, Jerry," she said. "I've just been reading in the paper how you organised the plan for getting rid of them. I think it was just wonderful of you."

A little time ago I'd probably have taken that for a cue, but it was no trigger now. I sort of kept on seeing her with her arms full of twins, and wondering in a dead-inside way how they got there.

"There wasn't a lot to it, darling," I told her modestly. "Anyone else might have hit on the idea."

"That's as maybe – but a whole lot of people don't think so. And I'll tell you another thing I heard today. They're going to ask you to stand for the Council, Jerry."

"Me on the Council. That'd be a big laugh—" I began. Then I stopped suddenly. "If – I mean, would that mean I'd be called 'Councillor'?" I asked her.

"Why – well, yes, I suppose so," she said, looking puzzled.

Things shimmered a bit.

"Er – Sally, darling – er, sweetheart, there's – er – something I've been trying to get round to saying to you for quite a time . . ." I began.

Light of Other Days

BOB SHAW

Leaving the village behind, we followed the heady sweeps of the road up into a land of slow glass.

I had never seen one of the farms before and at first found them slightly eerie – an effect heightened by imagination and circumstance. The car's turbine was pulling smoothly and quietly in the damp air so that we seemed to be carried over the convolutions of the road in a kind of supernatural silence. On our right the mountain sifted down into an incredibly perfect valley of timeless pine, and everywhere stood the great frames of slow glass, drinking light. An occasional flash of afternoon sunlight on their wind bracing created an illusion of movement, but in fact the frames were deserted. The rows of windows had been standing on the hillside for years, staring into the valley, and men only cleaned them in the middle of the night when their human presence would not matter to the thirsty glass.

They were fascinating, but Selina and I didn't mention the windows. I think we hated each other so much we both were reluctant to sully anything new by drawing it into the nexus of our emotions. The holiday, I had begun to realise, was a stupid idea in the first place. I had thought it would cure everything, but, of course, it didn't stop Selina being pregnant and, worse still, it didn't even stop her being angry about being pregnant.

Rationalising our dismay over her condition, we had circulated the usual statements to the effect that we would have *liked* having children – but later on, at the proper time. Selina's pregnancy had cost us her well-paid job and with it the new house we had been negotiating and which was far beyond the reach of my income from poetry. But the real source of our annoyance was that we were face to face with the realisation that people who say they want children later always mean they want children never. Our nerves were thrumming with the knowledge that we, who had thought ourselves so unique, had fallen into the same biological trap as every mindless rutting creature which ever existed.

The road took us along the southern slopes of Ben Cruachan until we began to catch glimpses of the grey Atlantic far ahead. I had just cut our speed to absorb the view better when I noticed the sign spiked to a gatepost. It said: "SLOW GLASS – Quality High, Prices Low – J. R. Hagan." On an impulse I stopped the car on the verge, wincing slightly as tough grasses whipped noisily at the bodywork.

"Why have we stopped?" Selina's neat, smoke-silver head turned in surprise.

"Look at that sign. Let's go up and see what there is. The stuff might be reasonably priced out here."

Selina's voice was pitched high with scorn as she refused, but I was too taken with my idea to listen. I had an illogical conviction that doing something extravagant and crazy would set us right again.

"Come on," I said, "the exercise might do us some good. We've been driving too long anyway."

She shrugged in a way that hurt me and got out of the car. We walked up a path made of irregular packed clay steps nosed with short lengths of sapling. The path curved through trees which clothed the edge of the hill and at its end we found a low farmhouse. Beyond the little stone building tall frames of slow glass gazed out towards the voice-stilling sight of Cruachan's ponderous descent towards the waters of Loch Linnhe. Most of the panes were perfectly transparent but a few were dark, like panels of polished ebony.

As we approached the house through a neat cobbled yard a tall middle-aged man in ash-coloured tweeds arose and waved to us. He had been sitting on the low rubble wall which bounded the yard, smoking a pipe and staring towards the house. At the front window of the cottage a young woman in a tangerine dress stood with a small boy in her arms, but she turned disinterestedly and moved out of sight as we drew near.

"Mr Hagan?" I guessed.

"Correct. Come to see some glass, have you? Well, you've come to the right place." Hagan spoke crisply, with traces of the pure Highland which sounds so much like Irish to the unaccustomed ear. He had one of those calmly dismayed faces one finds on elderly road-menders and philosophers.

"Yes," I said. "We're on holiday. We saw your sign."

Selina, who usually has a natural fluency with strangers, said nothing. She was looking towards the now empty window with what I thought was a slightly puzzled expression.

"Up from London, are you? Well, as I said, you've come to the right place – and at the right time, too. My wife and I don't see many people this early in the season."

I laughed. "Does that mean we might be able to buy a little glass without mortgaging our home?"

"Look at that now," Hagan said, smiling helplessly. "I've thrown away any advantage I might have had in the transaction. Rose, that's my wife, says I never learn. Still, let's sit down and talk it over." He pointed at the rubble wall, then glanced doubtfully at Selina's immaculate blue skirt. "Wait till I fetch a rug from the house." Hagan limped quickly into the cottage, closing the door behind him.

"Perhaps it wasn't such a marvellous idea to come up here," I whispered to Selina, "but you might at least be pleasant to the man. I think I can smell a bargain."

"Some hope," she said with deliberate coarseness. "Surely even you must have noticed that ancient dress his wife is wearing? He won't give much away to strangers."

"Was that his wife?"

"Of course that was his wife."

"Well, well," I said, surprised. "Anyway, try to be civil with him. I don't want to be embarrassed."

Selina snorted, but she smiled whitely when Hagan reappeared and I relaxed a little. Strange how a man can love a woman and yet at the same time pray for her to fall under a train.

Hagan spread a tartan blanket on the wall and we sat down, feeling slightly self-conscious at having been translated from our city-orientated lives into a rural tableau. On the distant slate of the Loch, beyond the watchful frames of slow glass, a slow-moving steamer drew a white line towards the south. The boisterous mountain air seemed almost to invade our lungs, giving us more oxygen than we required.

"Some of the glass farmers around here," Hagan began, "give strangers, such as yourselves, a sales talk about how beautiful the autumn is in this part of Argyll. Or it might be the spring, or the winter. I don't do that – any fool knows that a place which doesn't look right in the summer never looks right. What do you say?"

I nodded compliantly.

"I want you just to take a good look out towards Mull, Mr . . . "

"Garland."

" . . . Garland. That's what you're buying if you buy my glass, and it never looks better than it does at this minute. The glass is in perfect phase, none of it is less than ten years thick – and a four-foot window will cost you 200 pounds."

"*Two hundred!*" Selina was shocked. "That's as much as they charge at the Scenedow shop in Bond Street."

Hagan smiled patiently, then looked closely at me to see if I knew enough about slow glass to appreciate what he had been saying. His price had been much higher than I had hoped – but *ten years thick*! The cheap glass one found in places like the Vistaplex and Pane-o-rama stores usually consisted of a quarter of an inch of ordinary glass faced with a veneer of slow glass perhaps only ten or twelve months thick.

"You don't understand, darling," I said, already determined to buy. "This glass will last ten years and it's in phase."

"Doesn't that only mean it keeps time?"

Hagan smiled at her again, realising he had no further necessity to bother with me. "Only, you say! Pardon me, Mrs Garland, but you don't seem to appreciate the miracle, the genuine honest-to-goodness miracle, of engineering precision needed to produce a piece of glass in phase. When I say the glass is ten years thick it means it takes light ten years to pass through it. In effect, each one of those panes is ten light-years thick – more than twice the distance to the nearest star – so a variation in actual thickness of only a millionth of an inch would . . . "

He stopped talking for a moment and sat quietly looking towards the house. I turned my head from the view of the Loch and saw the young woman standing at the window again. Hagan's eyes were filled with a kind of greedy reverence which made me feel uncomfortable and at the same time convinced me Selina had been wrong. In my experience husbands never looked at wives that way, at least, not at their own.

The girl remained in view for a few seconds, dress glowing warmly, then moved back into the room. Suddenly I received a distinct, though inexplicable, impression she was blind. My feeling was that Selina and I were perhaps blundering through an emotional interplay as violent as our own.

"I'm sorry," Hagan continued, "I thought Rose was going to call me for something. Now, where was I, Mrs Garland? Ten light-years compressed into a quarter of an inch means . . . "

I ceased to listen, partly because I was already sold, partly because I had heard the story of slow glass many times before and had never yet understood the principles involved. An acquaintance with scientific training had once tried to be helpful by telling me to visualise a pane of slow glass as a hologram which did not need coherent light from a laser for the reconstitution of its visual information, and in which every photon of ordinary light passed through a spiral tunnel coiled outside the radius of capture of each atom in the glass. This gem of, to me, incomprehensibility not only told me nothing, it convinced me once again that a mind as non-technical as mine should concern itself less with causes than effects.

The most important effect, in the eyes of the average individual, was that light took a long time to pass through a sheet of slow glass. A new piece was always jet black because nothing had yet come through, but one could stand the glass beside, say, a woodland lake until the scene emerged, perhaps a year later. If the glass was then removed and installed in a dismal city flat, the flat would – for that year – appear to overlook the woodland lake. During the year it wouldn't be merely a very realistic but still picture – the water would ripple in sunlight, silent animals would come to drink, birds would cross the sky, night would follow day, season would follow season. Until one day, a year later, the beauty held in the subatomic pipelines would be exhausted and the familiar grey city-scape would reappear.

Apart from its stupendous novelty value, the commercial success of slow glass was founded on the fact that having a scenedow was the exact emotional equivalent of owning land. The meanest cave dweller could look out on misty parks – and who was to say they weren't his? A man who really owns tailored gardens and estates doesn't spend his time proving his ownership by crawling on his ground, feeling, smelling, tasting it. All he receives from the land are light patterns, and with scenedows those patterns could be taken into coal mines, submarines, prison cells.

On several occasions I have tried to write short pieces about the enchanted crystal but, to me, the theme is so ineffably poetic as to be, paradoxically, beyond the reach of poetry – mine at any rate. Besides, the best songs and verse had already been written, with prescient inspiration, by men who had died long before slow glass was discovered. I had no hope of equalling, for example, Moore with his:

Oft in the stilly night,
Ere slumber's chain has bound me,

Light of Other Days

Fond Memory brings the light,
Of other days around me . . .

It took only a few years for slow glass to develop from a scientific curiosity to a sizeable industry. And much to the astonishment of us poets – those of us who remain convinced that beauty lives though lilies die – the trappings of that industry were no different from those of any other. There were good scenedows which cost a lot of money, and there were inferior scenedows which cost rather less. The thickness, measured in years, was an important factor in the cost but there was also the question of *actual* thickness, or phase.

Even with the most sophisticated engineering techniques available thickness control was something of a hit-and-miss affair. A coarse discrepancy could mean that a pane intended to be five years thick might be five and half, so that light which entered in summer emerged in winter; a fine discrepancy could mean that noon sunshine emerged at midnight. These incompatibilities had their peculiar charm – many night workers, for example, liked having their own private time zones – but, in general, it cost more to buy scenedows which kept closely in step with real time.

Selina still looked unconvinced when Hagan had finished speaking. She shook her head almost imperceptibly and I knew he had been using the wrong approach. Quite suddenly the pewter helmet of her hair was disturbed by a cool gust of wind, and huge clean tumbling drops of rain began to spang round us from an almost cloudless sky.

"I'll give you a cheque now," I said abruptly, and saw Selina's green eyes triangulate angrily on my face. "You can arrange delivery?"

"Aye, delivery's no problem," Hagan said, getting to his feet. "But wouldn't you rather take the glass with you?"

"Well, yes – if you don't mind." I was shamed by his readiness to trust my scrip.

"I'll unclip a pane for you. Wait here. It won't take long to slip it into a carrying frame." Hagan limped down the slope towards the seriate windows, through some of which the view towards Linnhe was sunny, while others were cloudy and a few pure black.

Selina drew the collar of her blouse closed at her throat. "The least he could have done was invite us inside. There can't be so many fools passing through that he can afford to neglect them."

I tried to ignore the insult and concentrated on writing the cheque. One of the outsize drops broke across my knuckles, splattering the pink paper.

"All right," I said, "let's move in under the eaves till he gets back." You worm, I thought as I felt the whole thing go completely wrong. I just had to be a fool to marry you. A prize fool, a fool's fool – and now that you've trapped part of me inside you I'll never ever, never ever, *never ever* get away.

Feeling my stomach clench itself painfully, I ran behind Selina to the side of the cottage. Beyond the window the neat living room, with its coal fire, was empty but the child's toys were scattered on the floor. Alphabet blocks and a wheelbarrow the exact colour of fresh pared carrots. As I stared in, the boy came running from the other room and began kicking the blocks. He didn't notice me. A few moments later the young woman entered the room and lifted him, laughing easily and whole-heartedly as she swung the boy under her arm. She came to the window as she had done earlier. I smiled self-consciously, but neither she nor the child responded.

My forehead prickled icily. *Could they both be blind?* I sidled away.

Selina gave a little scream and I spun towards her.

"The rug!" she said. "It's getting soaked."

She ran across the yard in the rain, snatched the reddish square from the dappling wall and ran back, towards the cottage door. Something heaved convulsively in my subconscious.

"Selina," I shouted. "Don't open it!"

But I was too late. She had pushed open the latched wooden door and was standing, hand over mouth, looking into the cottage. I moved close to her and took the rug from her unresisting fingers.

As I was closing the door I let my eyes traverse the cottage's interior. The neat living room in which I had just seen the woman and child was, in reality, a sickening clutter of shabby furniture, old newspapers, cast-off clothing and smeared dishes. It was damp, stinking and utterly deserted. The only object I recognised from my view through the window was the little wheelbarrow, paintless and broken.

I latched the door firmly and ordered myself to forget what I had seen. Some men who live alone are good housekeepers; others just don't know how.

Selina's face was white. "I don't understand. I don't understand it."

"Slow glass works both ways," I said gently. "Light passes out of a house, as well as in."

"You mean . . . ?"

"I don't know. It isn't our business. Now steady up – Hagan's coming back with our glass." The churning in my stomach was beginning to subside.

Hagan came into the yard carrying an oblong, plastic-covered frame. I held the cheque out to him, but he was staring at Selina's face. He seemed to know immediately that our uncomprehending fingers had rummaged through his soul. Selina avoided his gaze. She was old and ill-looking, and her eyes stared determinedly towards the nearing horizon.

"I'll take the rug from you, Mr Garland," Hagan finally said. "You shouldn't have troubled yourself over it."

"No trouble. Here's the cheque."

"Thank you." He was still looking at Selina with a strange kind of supplication. "It's been a pleasure to do business with you."

"The pleasure was mine," I said with equal, senseless formality. I picked up the heavy frame and guided Selina towards the path which led to the road. Just as we reached the head of the now slippery steps Hagan spoke again.

"Mr Garland!"

I turned unwillingly.

"It wasn't my fault," he said steadily. "A hit-and-run driver got them both, down on the Oban road six years ago. My boy was only seven when it happened. I'm entitled to keep something."

I nodded wordlessly and moved down the path, holding my wife close to me, treasuring the feel of her arms locked around me. At the bend I looked back through the rain at Hagan sitting with squared shoulders on the wall where we had first seen him.

He was looking at the house, but I was unable to tell if there was anyone at the window.

Time Has No Boundaries

JACK FINNEY

On one of the upper floors of the new Hall of Justice I found the room number I was looking for, and opened the door. A nice-looking girl inside glanced up from her typewriter, switched on a smile, and said, "Professor Weygand?" It was a question in form only – one glance at me, and she knew – and I smiled and nodded, wishing I'd worn my have-fun-in-San-Francisco clothes instead of my professor's outfit. She said, "Inspector Ihren's on the phone; would you wait, please?" and I nodded and sat down, smiling benignly the way a professor should.

My trouble is that, although I have the thin, intent, professorial face, I'm a little young for my job, which is assistant professor of physics at a large university. Fortunately I've had some premature grey in my hair ever since I was nineteen, and on campus I generally wear those miserable permanently baggy tweeds that professors are supposed to wear, though a lot of them cheat and don't. These suits, together with round, metal-rimmed, professor-style glasses which I don't really need, and a careful selection of burlap neckties in diseased plaids of bright orange, baboon blue, and gang green (*de rigueur* for gap-pocketed professor suits) complete the image. That's a highly popular word meaning that if you ever want to become a full professor you've got to quit looking like an undergraduate.

I glanced around the little anteroom: yellow plaster walls; a big calendar; filing cabinets; a desk, typewriter, and girl. I watched her the way I inspect some of my more advanced girl students – from under the brows and with a fatherly smile in case she looked up and caught me. What I really wanted to do, though, was pull out Inspector Ihren's letter and read it again for any clue I might have missed about why he wanted to see me. But I'm a little afraid of the police – I get a feeling of guilt just asking a cop a street direction – and I thought rereading the letter just now would betray my nervousness to Miss Candyhips here who would somehow secretly signal the inspector. I knew exactly what it said, anyway. It was a formally polite three-line request, addressed to my office on the campus, to come here and see Inspector Martin O. Ihren, if I would, at my convenience, if I didn't mind, please, sir. I sat wondering what he'd have done if, equally politely, I'd refused, when a buzzer buzzed, the smile turned on again, and the girl said, "Go right in, Professor." I got up, swallowing nervously, opened the door beside me, and walked into the Inspector's office.

Behind his desk he stood up slowly and reluctantly as though he weren't at all sure but what he'd be throwing me into a cell soon. He put out a hand suspiciously and without a smile, saying, "Nice of you to come." I answered, sat down before his desk, and I thought I knew what would have happened if I'd refused this man's invitation. He'd simply have arrived in my classroom, clapped on the handcuffs, and dragged me here. I don't mean that his face was forbidding or in any way remarkable; it looked ordinary enough. So did his brown hair and so did his plain grey suit. He was a young-middle-aged man somewhat taller and heavier than I was, and his eyes looked absolutely uninterested in anything in the universe but his work. I had the certain conviction that, except for crime news, he read nothing, not even newspaper headlines; that he was intelligent, shrewd, perceptive, and humourless; and that he probably knew no one but other policemen and didn't think much of most of them. He was an undistinguished formidable man, and I knew my smile looked nervous.

He got right to the point; he was more used to arresting

people than dealing with them socially. He said, "There's some people we can't find, and I thought maybe you could help us." I looked politely puzzled but he ignored it. "One of them worked in Haring's Restaurant; you know the place; been there for years. He was a waiter and he disappeared at the end of a three-day weekend with their entire receipts – nearly five thousand bucks. Left a note saying he liked Haring's and enjoyed working there but they'd been underpaying him for ten years and now he figured they were even. Guy with an oddball sense of humour, they tell me." Ihren leaned back in his swivel chair, and frowned at me. "We can't find that man. He's been gone over a year now, and not a trace of him."

I thought he expected me to say something, and did my best. "Maybe he moved to some other city, and changed his name."

Ihren looked startled, as though I'd said something even more stupid than he expected. "That wouldn't help!" he said irritatedly.

I was tired of feeling intimidated. Bravely I said, "Why not?"

"People don't steal in order to hole up forever; they steal money to spend it. His money's gone now, he feels forgotten, and he's got a job again somewhere – as a waiter." I looked sceptical, I suppose, because Ihren said, "Certainly as a waiter; he won't change jobs. That's all he knows, all he can do. Remember John Carradine, the movie actor? Used to see him a lot. Had a face a foot long, all chin and long jaw; very distinctive." I nodded, and Ihren turned in his swivel chair to a filing cabinet. He opened a folder, brought out a glossy sheet of paper, and handed it to me. It was a police WANTED poster, and while the photograph on it did not really resemble the movie actor it had the same remarkable long-jawed memorability. Ihren said, "He could move and he could change his name, but he could never change that face. Wherever he is he should have been found months ago; that poster went everywhere."

I shrugged, and Ihren swung to the file again. He brought out, and handed me, a large old-fashioned sepia photograph mounted on heavy grey cardboard. It was a group photo of a kind you seldom see any more – all the employees of a small business lined up on the sidewalk before it. There were a dozen moustached men in this and a woman in a long dress smiling and squinting in the sun as they stood before a small building which I recognised. It was Haring's Restaurant looking not too different than it does now. Ihren said, "I spotted this on the wall of the restaurant office; I don't suppose anyone has really looked at it in years. The big guy in the middle is the original owner who started the restaurant in 1885 when this was taken; no one knows who anyone else in the picture was but take a good look at the other faces."

I did, and saw what he meant; a face in the old picture almost identical with the one in the WANTED poster. It had the same astonishing length, the broad chin seeming nearly as wide as the cheekbones, and I looked up at Ihren. "Who is it? His father? His grandfather?"

Almost reluctantly he said, "Maybe. It could be, of course. But he sure looks like the guy we're hunting for, doesn't he? And look how he's grinning! Almost as though he'd deliberately gotten a job in Haring's Restaurant again, and were back in 1885 laughing at me!"

I said, "Inspector, you're being extremely interesting, not to say downright entertaining. You've got my full attention, believe me, and I am in no hurry to go anywhere else. But I don't quite see . . . "

"Well, you're a professor, aren't you? And professors are smart, aren't they? I'm looking for help anywhere I can get it. We've got half a dozen unsolved cases like that – people that absolutely should have been found, and found easy! William Spangler Greeson is another one; you ever heard of him?"

"Sure. Who hasn't in San Francisco?"

"That's right, big society name. But did you know he didn't have a dime of his own?"

I shrugged. "How should I know? I'd have assumed he was rich."

"His wife is; I suppose that's why he married her, though

they tell me she chased him. She's older than he is, quite a lot. Disagreeable woman; I've talked to her. He's a young, handsome, likeable guy, they say, but lazy; so he married her."

"I've seen him mentioned in Herb Caen's column. Had something to do with the theatre, didn't he?"

"Stage-struck all his life; tried to be an actor and couldn't make it. When they got married she gave him the money to back a play in New York, which kept him happy for a while; used to fly East a lot for rehearsals and out-of-town tryouts. Then he started getting friendly with some of the younger stage people, the good-looking female ones. His wife punished him like a kid. Hustled him back here, and not a dime for the theatre from then on. Money for anything else but he couldn't even buy a ticket to a play any more; he'd been a bad boy. So he disappeared with a hundred and seventy thousand bucks of hers, and not a sign of him since, which just isn't natural. Because he can't – you understand, he *can't* – keep away from the theatre. He should have shown up in New York long since – with a fake name, dyed hair, a moustache, some such nonsense. We should have had him months ago but we haven't; he's gone, too." Ihren stood up. "I hope you meant it when you said you weren't in a hurry, because . . . "

"Well, as a matter of fact . . . "

" . . . because I made an appointment for both of us. On Powell Street near the Embarcadero. Come on." He walked out from behind his desk, picking up a large manilla envelope lying on one corner of it. There was a New York Police Department return address on the envelope, I saw, and it was addressed to him. He walked to the door without looking back as though he knew I'd follow. Down in front of the building he said, "We can take a cab; with you along I can turn in a chit for it. When I went by myself I rode the cable car."

"On a day like this anyone who takes a cab when he can ride the cable car is crazy enough to join the police force."

Ihren said, "Okay, tourist," and we walked all the way up to Market and Powell in silence. A cable car had just been swung around on its turntable, and we got an outside seat, no one near us; presently the car began crawling and changing leisurely up Powell. You can sit outdoors on the cable cars, you know, and it was nice out, plenty of sun and blue sky, a typical late summer San Francisco day. But Ihren might as well have been on the New York subway. "So where is William Spangler Greeson?" he said as soon as he'd paid our fares. "Well, on a hunch I wrote the New York police, and they had a man put in a few hours for me at the city historical museum." Ihren opened his manilla envelope, pulled out several folded sheets of greyish paper, and handed the top one to me. I opened it; it was a photostatic copy of an old-style playbill, narrow and long. "Ever hear of that play?" Ihren said, reading over my shoulder. The sheet was headed: TONIGHT & ALL WEEK! SEVEN GALA NIGHTS! Below that, in big type: MABLE'S GREENHORN UNCLE!

"Sure, who hasn't?" I said. "Shakespeare, isn't it?" We were passing Union Square and the St Francis Hotel.

"Save the jokes for your students, and read the cast of characters."

I read it, a long list of names; there were nearly as many people in old-time plays as in the audiences. At the bottom of the list it said *Members of the Street Crowd*, followed by a dozen or more names in the middle of which appeared William Spangler Greeson.

Ihren said, "That play was given in 1906. Here's another from the winter of 1901." He handed me a second photostat, pointing to another listing at the bottom of the cast. *Onlookers at the Big Race*, this one said, and it was followed by a half-inch of names in small type, the third of which was William Spangler Greeson. "I've got copies of two more playbills," Ihren said, "one from 1902, the other from 1904, each with his name in the cast,"

The car swung off Powell, and we hopped off, and continued walking north on Powell. Handing back the photostat, I said, "It's his grandfather. Probably Greeson inherited his interest in the stage from him."

"You're finding a lot of grandfathers today, aren't you,

Professor?" Ihren was replacing the stats in their envelopes.

"And what are you finding, Inspector?"

"I'll show you in a minute," he said, and we walked on in silence. We could see the Bay up ahead now, beyond the end of Powell Street, and it looked beautiful in the sun, but Inspector Ihren didn't look at it. We were beside a low concrete building, and he gestured at it with his chin; a sign beside the door read STUDIO SIXTEEN: COMMERCIAL TV. We walked in, passed through a small office in which no one was present and into an enormous concrete-floored room in which a carpenter was building a set – the front wall of a little cottage. On through that room – the Inspector had obviously been here before – then he pulled open a pair of double doors, and we walked into a tiny movie theatre. There was a blank screen up front, a dozen seats, and a projection booth. From the booth a man's voice called, "Inspector?"

"Yeah. You ready?"

"Soon as I thread up."

"Okay." Ihren motioned me to a seat, and sat down beside me. Conversationally he said, "There used to be a minor character around town name of Tom Veeley, a sports fan, a nut. Went to every fight, every Giant and Forty-Niners game, every auto race, roller derby, and jai-alai exhibition that came to town – and complained about them all. We knew him because every once in a while he'd leave his wife. She hated sports, she'd nag him, he'd leave, and we'd have to pick him up on her complaint for desertion and nonsupport; he never got far away. Even when we'd nab him all he'd talk about was how sports were dead, the public didn't care any more and neither did the players, and he wished he'd been around in the really great days of sports. Know what I mean?"

I nodded, the tiny theatre went dark, and a beam of sharp white light flashed out over our heads. Then a movie appeared on the screen before us. It was black and white, square in shape, the motion somewhat more rapid and jerky than we're used to, and it was silent. There wasn't even any music, and it was eerie to watch the movement hearing no sound but the whir of the projector. The picture was a view of Yankee Stadium taken from far back of third base showing the stands, a man at bat, the pitcher winding up. Then it switched to a closeup – Babe Ruth at the plate, bat on shoulder, wire back-stop in the background, fans behind it. He swung hard, hit the ball, and – chin rising as he followed its flight – he trotted forward. Grinning, his fists pumping rhythmically, he jogged around the bases. Type matter flashed onto the screen: *The Babe does it again!* it began, and went on to say that this was his fifty-first home run of the 1927 season, and that it looked as though Ruth would set a new record.

The screen went blank except for some meaningless scribbled numbers and perforations flying past, and Ihren said, "A Hollywood picture studio arranged this for me, no charge. Sometimes they film cops-and-crooks television up here, so they like to cooperate with us."

Jack Dempsey suddenly appeared on the screen, sitting on a stool in a ring corner, men working over him. It was a poor picture; the ring was outdoors and there was too much sun. But it was Dempsey, all right, maybe twenty-four years old, unshaven and scowling. Around the edge of the ring, the camera panning over them now between rounds, sat men in flat-topped straw hats and stiff collars; some had handkerchiefs tucked into their collars and others were mopping their faces. Then, in the strange silence, Dempsey sprang up and moved out into the ring, crouching very low, and began sparring with an enormous slow-moving opponent; Jess Willard, I imagined. Abruptly the picture ended, the screen illuminated with only a flickering white light. Ihren said, "I looked through nearly six hours of stuff like this; everything from Red Grange to Gertrude Ederle. I pulled out three shots; here's the last one."

On the screen the scratched flickering film showed a golfer sighting for a putt; spectators stood three and four deep around the edge of the green. The golfer smiled engagingly and began waggling his putter; he wore knickers well down below his knees and his hair was parted in the middle and combed straight back. It was Bobby Jones, one of the world's great golfers, at the height of his career back in the 1920s. He tapped the ball, it rolled, dropped into the cup, and Jones hurried after it as the crowd broke onto the green to follow him – all except one man. Grinning, one man walked straight toward the camera, then stopped, doffed his cloth cap in a kind of salute, and bowed from the waist. The camera swung past him to follow Jones who was stooping to retrieve his ball. Then Jones moved on, the man who had bowed to us hurrying after him with the crowd, across the screen and out of sight forever. Abruptly the picture ended, and the ceiling lights came on.

Ihren turned to face me. "That was Veeley," he said, "and it's no use trying to convince me it was his grandfather, so don't try. He wasn't even born when Bobby Jones was winning golf championships, but just the same that was absolutely and indisputably Tom Veeley, the sports fan who's been missing from San Francisco for six months now." He sat waiting, but I didn't reply; what could I say to that? Ihren went on, "He's also sitting just back of home plate behind the screen when Ruth hit the home run, though his face is in shadow. And I think he's one of the men mopping his face at ringside during the Dempsey fight, though I'm not absolutely certain."

The projection-booth door opened, the projectionist came out, saying, "That all today, Inspector?" and Ihren said yeah. The projectionist glanced at me, said, "Hi, Professor," and left.

Ihren nodded. "Yeah, he knows you, Professor. He remembers you. Last week when he ran off this stuff for me, we came to the Bobby Jones film. He remarked that he'd run that one off for someone else only a few days before. I asked who it was, and he said a professor from the university named Weygand. Professor, we must be the only two people in the world interested in that one little strip of film. So I checked on you; you were an assistant professor of physics, brilliant and with a fine reputation, but that didn't help me. You had no criminal record, not with us, anyway, but that didn't tell me anything either; most people have no criminal record, and at least half of them ought to. Then I checked with the newspapers, and the *Chronicle* had a clipping about you filed in their morgue. Come on" – Ihren stood up – "let's get out of here."

Outside, he turned toward the Bay, and we walked to the end of the street, then out onto a wooden pier. A big tanker, her red-painted bottom high out of the water, was sailing past, but Ihren didn't glance at her. He sat down on a piling, motioning me to another beside him, and pulled a newspaper clipping from his breast pocket. "According to this, you gave a talk before the American-Canadian Society of Physicists in June, 1961, at the Fairmont Hotel."

"Is that a crime?"

"Maybe; I didn't hear it. You spoke on 'Some Physical Aspects of Time,' the clipping says. But I don't claim I understood the rest."

"It was a pretty technical talk."

"I got the idea, though, that you thought it might actually be possible to send a man back to an earlier time."

I smiled. "Lots of people have thought so, including Einstein. It's a widely held theory. But that's all, Inspector; just a theory."

"Then let's talk about something that's more than a theory. For over a year San Francisco has been a very good market for old-style currency; I just found that out. Every coin and stamp dealer in town has had new customers, odd ones who didn't give their names and who didn't care what condition the old money was in. The more worn, dirty and creased – and therefore cheaper – the better they liked it, in fact. One of these customers, about a year ago, was a man with a remarkably long thin face. He bought bills and a few coins; any kind at all suited him just as long as they were no later than 1885. Another customer was a young, good-looking, agreeable guy who wanted bills no later than the early 1900s. And so on. Do you know why I brought you out on this dock?"

"No."

He gestured at the long stretch of empty pier behind us. "Because there's no one within a block of us; no witnesses. So tell me, Professor – I can't use what you say, uncorroborated, as evidence – how the hell did you do it? I think you'd like to tell someone; it might as well be me."

Astonishingly, he was right; I *did* want to tell someone, very much. Quickly, before I could change my mind, I said, "I use a little black box with knobs on it, brass knobs." I stopped, stared for a few seconds at a white Coast Guard cutter sliding into view from behind Angel Island, then shrugged and turned back to Ihren. "But you aren't a physicist; how can I explain? All I can tell you is that it really *is* possible to send a man into an earlier time. Far easier, in fact, than any of the theorists had supposed. I adjust the knobs, the dials, focusing the black box on the subject like a camera, as it were. Then" – I shrugged again – "well, I switch on a very faint specialised kind of precisely directed electric current or beam. And while my current is on – how shall I put it? He is afloat, in a manner of speaking; he is actually free of time, which moves on ahead without him. I've calculated that he is adrift, the past catching up with him at a rate of twenty-three years and eleven weeks for each second my current is on. Using a stopwatch, I can send a man back to whatever time he wishes with a plus or minus accuracy of three weeks. I know it works because – well, Tom Veeley is only one example. They all try to do something to show me they arrived safely, and Veeley said he'd do his best to get into the newsreel shot when Jones won the Open Golf Championship. I checked the newsreel last week to make sure he had."

The inspector nodded. "All right; now, *why* did you do it? They're criminals, you know; and you helped them escape."

I said, "No, I didn't know they were criminals, Inspector. And they didn't tell me. They just seemed like nice people with more troubles than they could handle. And I did it because I needed what a doctor needs when he discovers a new serum –

volunteers to try it! And I got them; you're not the only one who ever read that news report."

"Where'd you do it?"

"Out on the beach not far from the Cliff House. Late at night when no one was around."

"Why out there?"

"There's some danger a man might appear in a time and place already occupied by something else, a stone wall or building, his molecules occupying the same space. He'd be all mixed in with the other molecules, which would be unpleasant and confining. But there've never been any buildings on the beach. Of course the beach might have been a little higher at one time than another, so I took no chances. I had each of them stand on the lifeguard tower, appropriately dressed for whatever time he planned to enter, and with the right kind of money for the period in his pocket. I'd focus carefully around him so as to exclude the tower, turn on the current for the proper time, and he'd drop onto the beach of fifty, sixty, seventy, or eighty years ago."

For a while the inspector sat nodding, staring absently at the rough planks of the pier. Then he looked up at me again, vigorously rubbing his palms together. "All right, Professor, and now you're going to bring them all back!" I began shaking my head, and he smiled grimly and said, "Oh, yes, you are, or I'll wreck your career! I can do it, you know. I'll bring out everything I've told you, and I'll show the connections. Each of the missing people visited you more than once. Undoubtedly some of them were seen. You may even have been seen on the beach. Time I'm through, you'll never teach again." I was still shaking my head, and he said dangerously, "You mean you won't?"

"I mean I can't, you idiot! How the hell can I reach them? They're back in 1885, 1906, 1927, or whatever; it's absolutely impossible to bring them back. They've escaped you, Inspector – forever."

He actually turned white. "No!" he cried. "*No*; they're criminals and they've got to be punished, *got* to be!"

I was astounded. "Why? None of them's done any great harm. And as far as we're concerned, they don't exist. Forget them."

He actually bared his teeth. "Never," he whispered, then he roared, "I *never* forget a wanted man!"

"Okay, Javert."

"Who?"

"A fictional policeman in a book called *Les Misérables*. He spent half his life hunting down a man no one else wanted any more."

"Good man; like to have him in the department."

"He's not generally regarded too highly."

"He is by me!" Inspector Ihren began slowly pounding his fist into his palm, muttering, "They've got to be punished, they've got to be punished," then he looked up at me. "Get *out* of here," he yelled, "*fast!*" and I was glad to, and did. A block away I looked back, and he was still sitting there on the dock slowly pounding his fist in his palm.

I thought I'd seen the last of him then but I hadn't; I saw Inspector Ihren one more time. Late one evening about ten days later he phoned my apartment and asked me – ordered me – to come right over with my little black box, and I did even though I'd been getting ready for bed; he simply wasn't a man you disobeyed lightly. When I walked up to the big dark Hall of Justice he was standing in the doorway, and without a word he nodded at a car at the curb. We got in, and drove in silence out to a quiet little residential district.

The streets were empty, the houses dark; it was close to midnight. We parked just within range of a corner street light, and Ihren said, "I've been doing some thinking since I saw you last, and some research." He pointed to a mailbox beside the street lamp on the corner a dozen feet ahead. "That's one of the three mailboxes in the city of San Francisco that has been in the same location for almost ninety years. Not that identical box, of course, but always that location. And now we're going to mail some letters." From his coat pocket, Inspector Ihren brought out a little sheaf of envelopes, addressed in pen and ink, and stamped for mailing. He showed me the top one, shoving the others into his pocket. "You see who this is for?"

"The chief of police."

"That's right; the San Francisco chief of police – in 1885! That's his name, address, and the kind of stamp they used then. I'm going to walk to the mailbox on the corner, and hold this in the slot. You'll focus your little black box on the envelope, turn on the current as I let it go, and it will drop into the mailbox that stood here in 1885!"

I shook my head admiringly; it was ingenious. "And what does the letter say?"

He grinned evilly. "I'll tell you what it says! Every spare moment I've had since I last saw you, I've been reading old newspapers at the library. In December, 1884, there was a robbery, several thousand dollars missing; there isn't a word in the paper for months afterward that it was ever solved." He held up the envelope. "Well, this letter suggests to the chief of police that they investigate a man they'll find working in Haring's Restaurant, a man with an unusually long thin face. And that if they search his room, they'll probably find several thousand dollars he can't account for. And that he will absolutely *not* have an alibi for the robbery in 1884!" The Inspector smiled, if you could call it a smile. "That's all they'll need to send him to San Quentin, and mark the case closed; they didn't pamper criminals in those days!"

My jaw was hanging open. "But he isn't guilty! Not of that crime!"

"He's guilty of another just about like it! And he's got to be punished; I *will* not let him escape, not even to 1885!"

"And the other letters?"

"You can guess. There's one for each of the men you helped get away, addressed to the police of the proper time and place. And you're going to help me mail them all, one by one. If you don't I'll ruin you, and that's a promise, Professor." He opened his door, stepped out, and walked to the corner without even glancing back.

I suppose there are those who will say I should have refused to use my little black box no matter what the consequences to me. Well, maybe I should have, but I didn't. The inspector meant what he said and I knew it, and I wasn't going to have the only career I ever had or wanted be ruined. I did the best I could; I begged and pleaded. I got out of the car with my box; the inspector stood waiting at the mailbox. "*Please* don't make me do this," I said. "*Please!* There's no need! You haven't told anyone else about this, have you?"

"Of course not; I'd be laughed off the force."

"Then forget it! Why hound these poor people? They haven't done so much; they haven't really hurt anyone. Be humane! Forgiving! Your ideas are at complete odds with modern conceptions of criminal rehabilitation!"

I stopped for breath, and he said, "You through, Professor? I hope so, because nothing will ever change my mind. Now, go ahead and use that damn box!" Hopelessly I shrugged, and began adjusting the dials.

I am sure that the most baffling case the San Francisco Bureau of Missing Persons ever had will never be solved. Only two people – Inspector Ihren and I – know the answer, and we're not going to tell. For a short time there was a clue someone might have stumbled onto, but I found it. It was in the rare photographs section of the public library; they've got hundreds of old San Francisco pictures, and I went through them all and found this one. Then I stole it; one more crime added to the list I was guilty of hardly mattered.

Every once in a while I get it out, and look at it; it shows a row of uniformed men lined up in formation before a San Francisco police station. In a way it reminds me of an old movie comedy because each of them wears a tall helmet of felt with a broad turn-down brim, and long uniform coats to the knees. Nearly every one of them wears a drooping moustache, and each holds a long nightstick poised at the shoulder as though ready to bring it down on Chester Conklin's head. Keystone Kops they look like at first glance, but study those faces closely and you change your mind about that. Look especially close at the face of the man at the very end of the row, wearing sergeant's stripes. It looks positively and permanently ferocious, glaring out (or so it always seems) directly at me. It is the implacable face of Martin O. Ihren of the San Francisco police force, back where he really belongs, back where I sent him with my little black box, in the year 1893.

Alice's Godmother

WALTER DE LA MARE

Though Alice sat steadily looking out of the small square pane of glass in the railway carriage, she was not really seeing the green and hilly country through which the train now clattered on its way. While everything near – quickening hedges, grazing cattle, galloping calves, wood, farm and stony foaming brook – swept past far too swiftly for more than a darting glance; everything in the distance – hill, tree and spire – seemed to be stealthily wheeling forward, as if to waylay the puffing engine and prevent it from reaching her journey's end.

"If only it would!" sighed Alice to herself. "How much – much happier I should be!" Her blue eyes widened at the fancy. Then once more a frown of anxiety drew her eyebrows together; but she said nothing aloud. She sat on in her corner gently clasping her mother's hand and pondering in dismay on what might happen to her in the next few hours.

Alice and her mother a little prided themselves on being just "Two quiet ordinary people", happy in each other's company, and very seldom going out or paying calls and visits. And the particular visit that Alice was about to make when they reached the little country station of Freshing, she was to make alone. It was this that alarmed her. The invitation in that queer scrabbling handwriting had been to herself only. So though her mother was with her now, soon they would be parting. And every now and again Alice would give the hand she held in hers a gentle squeeze of self-reassurance. It was the Good-bye – though it would be only for a few hours – that she dreaded.

And yet their plans had all been talked over and settled again and again. Alice must, of course, take a fly from the station – whatever the expense. After telling the cabman when she would need him again, she would get into it and her mother would wait for her in a room at the village Inn until she herself returned in the early evening from her visit. Then everything would be safely over. And to imagine the joy of seeing all these fields and woods come racing back the other way round almost made Alice ill.

It was absurd to be so nervous. Alice had told herself that a hundred times. But it was no use. The very thought of her great-great-great-great-great-great-great-great-grandmother filled her heart with a continuous foreboding. If only she were a little stronger-minded; if only this old old lady, who was also her godmother, had asked her mother to come with her; if only her heart would stop beating so fast; if only a wheel would come off the engine!

But then, after all, Alice had never before so much as seen her godmother. Even now she could not be quite certain that she had the number of "greats" to the "grandmama" quite right. Not even strong-minded people, she supposed, are often suddenly invited to tea with relatives aged three-hundred-and-forty-nine. And not only that either; for this day – this very Saturday – was her godmother's birthday: her three-hundred-and-fiftieth!

Whenever Alice remembered this, a faint smile stole into her face. At seventeen a birthday is a real "event". Life is galloping on. You are sprouting up like a beanstalk. Your hair is "put up" (or at least it was when Alice was a girl), your skirts "come down", and you're soon to "come out". In other words you are beginning to be really and truly "grown-up". But three-hundred-and-fifty! Surely by that time . . . It must be difficult even to be certain you have the total right. Surely there can't be *any* kind of a change by then! Surely not!

Still, Alice thought, it is perhaps the *name* of the number that chiefly counts. She herself had known what an odd shock it had been to slip into her teens, and could guess what the shivers would be like of the plunge into her twenties. Yet even if it were only the name of the number – why, at the end of three centuries you must be beginning to be getting accustomed to birthdays.

It was a little odd that her godmother had never asked to see her before. Years ago she had sent her a squat parcel-gilt mug – a mug that her godmother herself used to drink her beer out of when she was a child of ten in Queen Elizabeth's reign. A little sheepskin, illuminated Prayer Book, too, that had once been given to her godmother by Charles the First, and a few exquisite little old gold trinkets had come too. But receiving presents is not the same thing as actually meeting and talking with the mysterious giver of them. It is one thing to imagine the unknown; another thing altogether to meet it face to face. What would her godmother look like? What *could* she look like? Alice hadn't the faintest notion. Old ladies of eighty and upwards are not unusual; but you can't just multiply eighty by four as if growing older were merely a sum in arithmetic.

Perhaps when you are very old indeed, Alice suspected, you have no wish to sit for a portrait or to be photographed. It is a petrifying experience even when you are young. When you are – well, very old indeed, you may prefer to – well, to keep yourself *to* yourself. *She* would.

"Mamma dear," she suddenly twisted round on her hard seat, her straight ribboned straw-coloured hair slipping over in one smooth ripple on her shoulder as she did so; "Mamma dear, I can't think even now what I ought to do when I go into the room. Will there be anybody there, do you think? Do I shake hands? I suppose she won't kiss me? I simply can't think what I ought to do. I shall just hate leaving you – being left, I mean."

She stroked hard with her fingers the hand that was in her own, and as she gazed at her mother's face in this increasing anxiety, she knew that the smile on it was just like a pretty blind over a window, and that her mother's self within was almost as much perturbed over this visit as she was herself.

"It's getting nearer, darling, at any rate, isn't it?" her mother whispered. "So it will sooner be over." Whereupon the fat old farmer in the further corner of the carriage emitted yet another grunt. He was fast asleep. "I *think*, " her mother continued softly, "I should first inquire of the maid if she is quite well – your godmother, I mean, my dear. Say, "Do you think Miss Cheyney is well enough to see me?" She will know what you ought to do. I am not even certain whether the poor old lady can speak: though her handwriting is simply marvellous."

"But, Mummie darling, how are we to know that there *will* be a maid? Didn't they, in godmother's time, always have 'retainers'? Supposing there are rows of them in the hall! And when ought I to get up to say Good-bye? If she is deaf and blind *and* dumb I really don't know what I *shall* do!"

A dozen questions at least like this had been asked but not answered during the last few days, and although Alice's cheek, with that light hair, was naturally pale, her mother watched it grow paler yet as the uncomfortable old-fashioned railway-carriage they sat in jogged steadily on its way.

"Whenever I am in any difficulty, sweetheart," she whispered close up to her daughter's ear, "I always say a little prayer."

"Yes, yes, dear dearest," said Alice, gazing at the fat old farmer, fast asleep. "But if only I weren't going quite alone! I don't think, you know, she can be a very good godmother: she never said a word in her letter about my Confirmation. She's at least old enough to know better." Once more the ghost of a smile stole softly over her face. But she clasped her mother's fingers even a little tighter, and the hedges and meadows continued to sidle by.

They said Good-bye to one another actually inside the cab, so as to be out of sight of the Inn and the cabman.

"I expect, my sweet," breathed Alice's mother, in the midst of this long embrace, "we shall both soon be smiling away like two turtledoves at the thought of all our worry. We can't tell what kind of things she may not be thinking of, can we? And don't forget, I shall be waiting for you in the 'Red Lion' – there's the sign, my dear, as you see. And if there is time, perhaps we will have a little supper there all to ourselves – a little soup, if they have it; or at any rate, an egg. I don't suppose you will have a very *substantial* tea. Not in the circumstances. But still, your godmother wouldn't have asked you to visit her if she had not really wanted to see you. We mustn't forget that, darling."

Alice craned her head out of the window till her mother was out of sight behind the hedge. And the fly rolled gently on and on and on along the dusty lanes in the direction of The Grange. On and on and on. Surely, thought Alice at last, we must have gone miles and miles. At this she sprang up and thrust her head out of the window, and called up to the cabman, "The Grange, you know, please."

"That's it, Miss, The Grange," he shouted back, with a flourish of his whip. "Not as how I can take you into the Park, Miss. It ain't allowed."

"Mercy me," sighed Alice as she sank back on the fusty blue cushions. "Supposing there are miles of avenue, and the front door's at the back!"

It was a pleasant sunny afternoon. The trim hedgerows were all in their earliest green; and the flowers of spring – primrose, violets, jack-in-the-hedge, stitchwort – in palest blossom starred the banks. It was only half-past three by Alice's little silver watch. She would be in good time, then. In a few minutes, indeed, the fly drew up beside immense rusty wrought-iron gates on the four posts of which stood heavy birds in stone, with lowered heads, brooding with outstretched wings.

"And you will be sure to come back for me at six?" Alice implored the cabman, though she tried to keep her voice natural and formal. "Not a minute later than six, please. And then wait here until I come."

The cabman ducked his head and touched his hat; drew his old horse round in the shafts, and off he went. Alice was alone.

With one last longing look at the strange though friendly country lane – and there was not a house in sight – Alice pushed open the little gate at the side of the two large ones. It emitted a faint, mocking squeal as it turned slowly upon its hinges. Beyond it rose a hedge of yew at least twenty feet high, and in a nook there stood a small square lodge, its windows shuttered, a scurry of dead leaves in its ancient porch. Alice came to a standstill. This was a difficulty neither she nor her mother had foreseen. Ought she to knock or go straight on? The house looked as blind as a bat. She stepped back, and glanced up at the chimneys. Not the faintest plume of smoke was visible against the dark foliage of the ilex behind the house. Some unseen bird flew into the shadows with a cry of alarm.

Surely the lodge was empty. None the less it might be good manners to make sure, so she stepped into the porch and knocked – but knocked in vain. After pausing a minute or two, and scanning once more the lifeless windows, in a silence broken only by the distant laughing of a woodpecker, Alice determined to go on.

So thick and close were the tufted mosses in the gravel of the narrow avenue that her footsteps made no sound. So deep was the shade cast by the immense trees that grew on either side she could have fancied evening was already come, though it was yet early afternoon. Mammoth beeches lifted their vast boughs into the air; the dark hollows in their ancient boles capacious enough for the dwelling-house of a complete family of humans. In the distance Alice could see between their branches gigantic cedars, and others still further, beneath which grazed what she supposed was a herd of deer, though it was impossible to be quite certain from so far.

The few wild creatures which had long ago detected her in these haunts were strangely tame. They did not trouble to run away; but turned aside and watched her as she passed, the birds hopping a little further out of her reach while yet continuing on their errands. In sheer curiosity indeed Alice made an attempt to get as near as she possibly could to a large buck rabbit that sat nibbling under the broken rail of the fence. With such success that he actually allowed her to scratch his furry head and stroke his long lopping ears.

"Well," thought she with a sigh as she straightened herself, "there can't be very much to be afraid of in great-great-great-great-great-great- great-great-grandmother's house if the rabbits are as tame as all that. *Au revoir,*" she whispered to the creature: "I hope to see you again very very soon." And on she went.

Now and then a hunchbacked thorn-tree came into view, and now and then a holly. Alice had heard long ago that hollies are wise enough not to grow prickles where no animal can damage their leaves by browsing on them. These hollies seemed to have no prickles at all, and the hawthorns, in spite of their bright green coats, speckled with tight buds, were almost as twisted out of shape as if mischievous little boys had tied knots in them when they were saplings. But how sweet was the tranquil air. So sweet indeed that this quiet avenue with its towering branches and the childlike blue of the skies overhead pacified her mind, and she had almost forgotten her godmother when, suddenly, at a break between the trees there came into view a coach.

Not exactly a coach, perhaps, but a large painted carriage of a faded vermilion and yellow, drawn by two cream-coloured horses – a coachman on the box in a mulberry livery, and a footman beside him. What was really strange, this conveyance was being noiselessly driven round a circular track so overgrown with moss and weeds that it was hardly discernible against the green of the grass. Alice could not but watch it come nearer and nearer – as she stood drawn up close to the furrowed bark of an oak that branched overhead. This must be her godmother's carriage. She must be taking her daily drive in concealment from the wide wide world. But no: it had drawn near; and now, with a glimpse of the faded red morocco within, it had passed; it was empty. Only the backs of coachman and footman now showed above its sun-bleached panels – their powdered hair, their cockaded hats.

All Alice's misgivings winged back into her mind at sight of this unusual spectacle. She tiptoed out of her hiding-place, and hastened on. Her one wish now was to reach her journey's end.

Presently after, indeed, the house itself appeared in sight. The shorn flowerless sward gently sloped towards its dark low walls and grey chimneys. To the right of it lay a pool as flat as a huge looking-glass in the frame of its trees. Behind it rose a smooth green hill.

Alice paused again behind yet another of the huge grey boles to scan it more closely before she herself could be spied out from any of its many windows. It looked as if it had stood there for ever. It looked as if its massive stones had of their own weight been sinking imperceptibly, century after century, into the ground. Not a blossoming shrub, not a flower near by – except only a powder of daisies and a few yellow dandelions.

Only green turf and trees, and the ancient avenue on which she stood, sweeping gently towards its low-porched entrance. "Well," she sighed to herself, "I'm thankful I don't live *there*, that's all – not even if I were a thousand-and-one!" She drew herself up, glanced at her shoes, gave a little push to her ribboned straw hat, and, with as much dignity as she could manage, proceeded straight onwards.

A hoarse bell responded, after a whole second's pause, to the gentle tug she had given the iron pull that hung in the porch. It cried "Ay, ay!" and fell silent. And Alice continued to look at the immense iron knocker which she hadn't the courage to use.

Without a sound the door opened at last, and there, as she had feared, stood, not a friendly parlour-maid with a neat laundered cap, but an old man in a black tail-coat who looked at her out of his pale grey eyes as if she were a stuffed bird in a glass case. Either he had been shrinking for some little time, or he must surely have put on somebody else's clothes, they hung so loosely on his shoulders.

"I am Miss Alice Cheyney – Miss Alice Cheyney," she said. "I think my great-great . . . Miss Cheyney is expecting me – that is, of course, if she is quite well." These few words had used up the whole of one breath, and her godmother's old butler continued to gaze at her, while they sank into his mind.

"Will you please to walk in," he said at last. "Miss Cheyney bade me express the wish that you will make yourself at home.

She hopes to be with you immediately." Whereupon he led the way, and Alice followed him – across a wide hall, lit with low, greenish, stone-mullioned windows. On either side stood suits of burnished armour, with lifted visors. But where the glittering eyes of their long-gone owners once had gleamed, nothing now showed but a little narrow darkness. After a hasty glance or two to either side, Alice kept her eyes fixed on the humped back of the little old butler. Up three polished stairs, under a hanging tapestry, he led her on, and at length, at the end of a long gallery, ushered her into what she supposed was her godmother's sitting-room. There, with a bow, he left her. Alice breathed one long deep sigh, and then, having unbuttoned and buttoned up again one of her grey silk gloves, she sat down on the edge of a chair near the door.

It was a long, low-pitched, but not very wide room, with a coffered ceiling and panelled walls, and never before had Alice seen such furniture. In spite of the dreadful shyness that seemed to fill her to the very brim, at thought of her mother's little pink-and-muslin drawing-room compared with this, she almost burst out laughing.

Make herself at home! Why, any one of those chests would hide her away for ever, like the poor lovely lost one in "The Mistletoe Bough". As for the hanging portraits in their great faded frames, though she guessed at once they must be by "old masters", and therefore eyed them as solemnly as she could, she had never supposed human beings could look so odd and so unfriendly. It was not so much their clothes: their stomachers, their slashed doublets and wide velvet caps, but their faces. Ladies with high bald foreheads and tapering fingers and thumb-rings, and men sour and dour and glowering.

"Oho! Miss Nobody!" they seemed to be saying. "And pray, what are *you* doing here?"

The one single exception was the drawing of a girl of about her own age. A dainty cap with flaps all but concealed her yellow hair; a necklet dangled at her breast; the primrose-coloured bodice sloped sharply to the waist. So delicate were the lines of this drawing and so faint the tinted chalk, they hardly stained the paper. Yet the eyes that gazed out across the low room at Alice seemed to be alight with life. A smile half-mocking, half-serious lingered in their depths. See, I am lovely, it seemed to be hinting, and yet how soon to be gone! And even though Alice had never before seen a face so enchanting, she could not but confess it bore a remote resemblance to herself. Why this should have a little restored her confidence she could not tell. None the less, she deliberately smiled back at the drawing as if to say, "Well, my dear, I shall have *you* on my side, whatever happens."

The lagging minutes ticked solemnly by. Not a sound to be heard in the great house; not a footfall. But at last a door at the further end of the room softly opened, and in the greenish light of the deep mullioned window appeared what Alice knew was She.

She was leaning smally on the arm of the butler who had admitted Alice to the house. Quiet as shadows they entered the room; then paused for a moment, while yet another manservant arranged a chair for his mistress. Meanwhile the old lady was peering steadily in search of her visitor. She must once have been as tall as Alice herself, but now time had shrunken her up into the stature of a child, and though her small head was set firmly on the narrow shoulders, these stooped like the wings of the morose stone birds upon her gates.

"Ah, is that you, my dear?" cried a voice; but so minute was the sound of these words that Alice went suddenly hot all over lest she had merely imagined them.

"I say, is that you, my dear?" repeated the voice. There was no mistaking now. Alice ventured a pace forward into the light, her knees trembling beneath her, and the old lady groped out a hand – its shrunken fingers closed one upon another like the cold claws of a bird.

For an instant Alice hesitated. The dreadful moment was come. Then she advanced, made the old lady a curtsy, and lifted the icy fingers to her lips.

"All I can say *is*," she confided to her mother when they met again, "all I can say *is*, Mamma, if it had been the Pope, I suppose I should have kissed his toe. And really, I would have very much rather."

None the less, Alice's godmother had evidently taken no offence at this gesture. Indeed what Alice thought might be a smile crinkled, as it were, across the exquisite web of wrinkles on her face. On her acorn-shaped head rose a high lace and silver cap resembling the gown she wore; and silk mittens concealed her wrists. She was so small that Alice had to bend almost double over her fingers. And when she was seated in her chair it was as if a large doll sat there – but a marvellous doll that had voice, thought, senses and motion beyond any human artificer's wildest fancy. The eyes in this dry wizened-up countenance – of a much fainter blue than the palest forget-me-not – steadily continued to look at Alice, the while the butler and footman with head inclined stood watching their mistress. Then, as if at a secret signal, they both bowed and retired.

"Be seated, my dear," the tinkling voice began when they had withdrawn. And there fell a horrifying pause. Alice gazed at the old lady, and like half-transparent glass the aged eyes remained fixed on herself, the bird-like hands crossed daintily over the square lace handkerchief held in the narrow lap. Alice grew hotter and hotter. "What a very beautiful old house this is, great-grandmamma," she suddenly blurted out. "And those wonderful trees!"

No flicker of expression showed that Miss Cheyney had heard what she had said. And yet Alice could not help thinking that she *had* heard, and that for some reason she had disapproved of her remark.

"Now come," piped the tiny voice, "now come; tell me what you have been doing this long time. And how is your mother? I think I faintly remember seeing her, my dear, soon after she married your father, Mr James Beaton."

"Mr Beaton, I *think*, was my great-grandfather, great-grandmamma," Alice breathed softly. "My father's name, you know, was John – John Cheyney."

"Ah well, your great-*grand*father, to be sure," said the old lady. "I never pay much attention to dates. And has anything been happening lately?"

"Happening, great-grandmamma?" echoed Alice.

"Beyond?" said the old lady. "in the world?"

Poor Alice; she knew well the experience of nibbling a pen over impossible questions in history examinations, but this was far worse than any she had ever encountered.

"There, you see!" continued her godmother. "I hear of the wonderful things they are doing, and yet when I ask a simple question like that no one has anything to say. Have you travelled on one of these steam railway trains yet? Locomotives?"

"I came that way this afternoon, great-grandmamma."

"Ah, I thought you looked a little flushed. The smoke must be most disagreeable."

Alice smiled. "No, thank you," she said kindly.

"And how is Queen Victoria?" said the old lady. "She is still alive?"

"Oh yes, great-grandmamma. And that is just, of course, what *has* been happening. It's her Diamond Jubilee this year – sixty years – you know."

"H'm," said the old lady. "Sixty. George III reigned sixty-three. But they all go in time. I remember my dear father coming up to my nursery after the funeral of poor young Edward VI. He was one of the Court pages, you know – that is, when Henry VIII was King. Such a handsome lad – there is his portrait . . . somewhere."

For a moment Alice's mind was a whirlpool of vague memories – memories of what she had read in her history-books.

But Miss Cheyney's bead-like notes had hardly paused. "You must understand that I have not asked you to come this long way by one of those horrid new-fangled steam-engines just to gossip about my childhood. Kings and Queens come and go like the rest of things. And though I have seen many changes, it seems to me the world is pretty much the same as ever. Nor can I believe that the newspaper is a beneficial novelty. When I was a girl we managed well enough without, and even in Mr Addison's day one small sheet twice a week was enough. But there, complaint is useless. And you cannot exactly be held responsible for all that. There were changes in my girlhood, too – great changes. The world was not so crowded then. There was nobility and beauty. Yes." Her eyes wandered, to rest a moment on the portrait of the young woman in the primrose gown. "The truth is, my dear," she continued, "I have to tell you something, and I wish you to listen."

Once more she remained silent a moment, clutching the handkerchief she held between her fingers. "What I desire you to tell *me*," she said at last, leaning stealthily forward in her great chair, "what I am anxious that you should tell me is, How long do you wish to live?"

For a few moments Alice sat cold and motionless. It was as if an icy breath straight from the North Pole had swept across the room, congealing with its horror the very air. Her eyes wandered vacantly from picture to picture, from ancient object to ancient object – aged, mute and lifeless – to rest at last on a flowering weed that reared its head beyond one of the diamond-shaped panes of glass in the window.

"I have never thought of that, great-grandmamma," her dry lips whispered. "I don't think I know."

"Well, I am not expecting an old head on young shoulders," retorted the old lady. "Perhaps if King Charles had realised that – so learned, so generous, so faithful a monarch – I doubt if that vulgar creature Oliver Cromwell would ever have succeeded in having his off."

The acorn chin drew down into its laces like a snail into its shell. Until this moment Alice might have been conversing with an exquisite image, or an automaton – the glittering eyes, the crooked fingers, the voice from afar. But now it seemed a new life was stirring in it. The tiny yet piercing tones sank almost to a whisper, the head stirred furtively from side to side as if to be sure no eavesdropper were within earshot.

"Now listen close to me, my child: I have a secret. A secret which I wish to share only with you. You would suppose, wouldn't you, that this being the three-hundred-and-fiftieth anniversary of my natal day" – and at this the dreadful realisation suddenly swept over Alice that she had quite forgotten to wish her godmother "Many happy returns" – "you might suppose that you are about to meet a gay numerous company here – young and happy creatures like yourself. But no: not so. Even your dear mother is, of course, only my great-great-great-great-great-great-great-granddaughter-*in-law*. She was a Miss Wilmot, I believe."

"Yes, Woodcot, great-grandmamma," said Alice softly.

"Well, Woodcot," said the old lady; "it is no matter. It is you, my child, whom I have made, to be precise, my chosen. In mere men I take no interest. Not only that, but you must now be of the age I was when the portrait you see on yonder wall was painted. It is the work of a pupil of Hans Holbein's. Hans Holbein himself, I believe, was dead at the time. Dear me, child, I remember sitting for that portrait in this very room – as if it were yesterday. It was much admired by Sir Walter Raleigh, who, you may remember, came to so unhappy an end. That was, I recollect, in my early seventies. My father and his father were boys together in Devonshire."

Alice blinked a little – she could not turn her eyes away from her godmother's – that mammet-like face, those minute motionless hands.

"Now glance at that picture, please!" the old lady bade her, pointing a tiny crooked-up forefinger towards the further wall. "Do you see any resemblance?"

Alice looked long and steadily at the portrait. But she had neither the courage nor vanity to deny that the fair smiling features were at least a *little* like her own. "To whom, great-grandmamma?" Alice whispered.

"To whom? Well, well, well!" came the reply, the words sounding like the chiming of a distant silver bell. "I see it. I see it . . . But never mind that now. Did you perhaps look at this *house* as you made your way up the avenue?"

"Oh yes, great-grandmamma – though I couldn't, of course, look close, you know," Alice managed to say.

"Did you *enjoy* its appearance?"

"I don't think I thought of that," said Alice. "The trees and park were very lovely. I have never seen such – *mature* trees, great-grandmamma. And yet all their leaves were budding and some were fully out. Isn't it wonderful for trees so – so long in the world to – why, to come out at all?"

"I was referring to the house," said the old lady. "*Springs* nowadays are not what they used to be. They have vanished from the England I once knew. I remember once an April when angels were seen on the hilltops above London. But that is no matter for us now: not now. The house?"

Once again Alice's gaze wandered – to come to rest again on the green, nodding weed at the window.

"It is a very very quiet house," she said.

The childlike tones died between the thick stone walls; and a profound silence followed them, like that of water in a well. Meanwhile, as Alice fully realised, her godmother had been fixedly searching her face with her remote but intent eyes. It was as if Time itself were only a child and that of this aged face he had made his little secret gazebo.

"Now please listen to me very carefully," she continued at last. "Such a countenance as yours – one bearing the least resemblance to that portrait over there, must be the possessor of a fair share of wits. I am old enough, my child, not to be charged, I hope, with the folly of vanity. In my girlhood I enjoyed a due share of admiration. And I have a proposal to make to you which will need all the sagacity you are capable of. Don't be alarmed. I have every faith in you. But first, I want you to go into the next room, where you will find a meal prepared. Young people nowadays, I hear, need continuous nourishment. What wonder! Since they have forgotten all the manners of a lady as *I* know them, and are never still for a moment together. What wonder! With all these dreadful machines I hear of, the discontent, the ignorance and folly, the noises and unrest and confusion. In my young days the poor were the poor and the humble the humble, my child; and knew their place. In my young days I would sit contented for hours at a time over a simple embroidery. And if I needed it, my mother never deigned to spare the rod. But there, I didn't invite you to visit an old woman merely to listen to a sermon. When you have refreshed yourself you are to take a little walk through the house. Go wherever you please; look well about you; no one will disturb you. And in an hour's time come back to me here again. Nowadays I take a little sleep in the afternoon. I shall be ready for you then . . . "

Alice, with a relief beyond words, rose from her chair. She curtsied again towards the small, motionless figure in the distance, and retired through the dark oak door.

The room in which she at once found herself was small, hexagonal, and panelled with the blackest of old oak. A copper candelabrum hung from the dark moulded ceiling, and beyond the leaded panes she could see the gigantic trees in the park. To her dismay the footman who had accompanied the butler into the room when her godmother had first made her appearance, was stationed behind the chair at the table. Never had Alice supposed that it was proper for men-servants, except perhaps gardeners, to wear long grey beards. But there he was, with his dim sidling eyes. And she must needs turn her back on him to seat herself at the table. She nibbled the fruit and bread, the rich cake and the sweetmeats which he presented in their heavy silver dishes, and she sipped her sweet drink. But it was a hasty and nervous meal, and she tasted nothing of what she had eaten.

As soon as it was over, the servant opened the door for her, and she began her voyage of discovery through the great, deserted house. It was as if her very ghost were her only company. Never had solitude so oppressed her, never before had she been so intensely aware of being wide awake and yet dreaming. The long corridors, the low and crooked lintelled doors, the dark uneven floors, their Persian mats, their tapestries and hangings, only the lovelier in that their colours had been dimmed by so many suns, the angled flights of stairs, the solemn air that brooded between the walls, the multitude of pictures, the huge beds, the endless succession of superannuated coffers, daybeds, cabinets – all this in but a few minutes had tired and fatigued Alice far more even than the long journey from the home of her childhood that morning. Upstairs and downstairs, on she wandered for all the world like the goosey-goosey-gander of the old nursery rhyme.

And when at last with a sigh she glanced at the bright little silver watch which had been her mother's birthday gift, its slender hands told her that she had still a full quarter-of-an-hour before she need return to her great-great-great-great-great-great-great-great-grandmother's room.

That into which she had now admitted herself seemed to be a small library. Its walls were ranged from ceiling to floor with old leather and lambskin folios and quartos and squat duodecimos, while between them hung portraits and the loveliest miniatures and medallions of scores upon scores of persons who she guessed must be her ancestors and ancestresses of goodness knows how many monarchs ago.

One or two of the pictures, indeed, as the crabbed inscriptions showed, had been gifts to the family from those monarchs themselves. In their various costumes, wigs, turbans and furbelows they looked as if they must have been the guests at an immense fancy-dress ball.

What tho Felicitie befal?
Time makyth shadowes of us all.

In this room a low recess filled the shallow bow window and on this lay a strip of tapestry. The leaded pane of the window was open. The sun was already westering, its beams slanting in on the gilt and ebony and ivory of the frames suspended from their nails. Alice knelt down at the window; and her mind slipped into a daydream, and her gaze wandered far away over the golden budding tops of the enormous oaks, the flat dark outstretched motionless palms of the cedars – perhaps descendants of those which Sir Philip Sidney had brought home to his beloved England from the East.

The thoughts that had all day been skittering in her mind like midges over a pool gradually fell still, and she sank deeper and deeper into the hush that lay over the ancient house. It was as if its walls were those of an enormous diving-bell sunken beyond measure in an unfathomable ocean of Time. So tranquil was the sweet April air beyond the window that she could actually detect the sound of the browsing of the herd of fallow deer that had now closely approached the lawns of the house itself.

And as, lost in this reverie, she sat entranced, she became conscious that a small living animal – the like of which she had never seen before – had crept up within a pace or two of her on the window-sill, and was now steadily regarding her with its clear bead-brown eyes. In size it was rather larger than a mole, its dark thick fur was soft as a beaver's, and it had a short, furry, and tufted tail. Its ears were cocked on its head, its silvery whiskers turned downwards above its jaws, and Alice could see its tiny ivory claws as it sat there erect on its haunches like a tame cat or a dog begging for a titbit of meat. Alice, alas, had nothing to offer her visitor, not even a cherry-stone, not even a crumb.

"Well, you pretty thing," she whispered, "what is it?"

The creature's whiskers moved ever so slightly, its eyes fixed more intently than ever on the face of this strange visitor. Very very delicately Alice thrust out her finger, and to her astonishment found herself gently caressing the furry nose. "It was as if I was in Wonderland, myself," she explained long afterwards to her mother. Perfectly mute and still, the owner of it seemed to enjoy this little courtesy. And when she had withdrawn her finger, it looked at her more closely and searchingly than ever, as if bidding her take heed. It then tapped repeatedly with its ivory-clawed paw on the oak casement, glanced searchingly at her yet again, then shook its furry head vehemently three times, paused, turned swiftly about and pattered away into hiding behind a huge carved Moorish cabinet before Alice could so much as bid it adieu.

Quiet little events in this life, even though we cannot understand what exactly they mean, are apt to *seem* to mean a great deal. So with this small animal and Alice. It was as if – though she was not aware of it – she had been brooding over a problem in Algebra or a proposition in Euclid, and it had ventured out of its living-place to tell her the answer. How fantastic a notion! – when Alice knew neither the problem nor what its solution was.

She glanced at her watch once more; her fair cheeks pinking all over at realising that she was now ten minutes late for her assignation with her grandmother. She must be gone. None the less, she had time to look her farewell at the huge dreaming park before she set out on her return journey.

Before at last finding her way, however, she irretrievably lost it. For the house was a silent maze of deceptive passages and corridors. Every fresh attempt only increased her confusion, and then suddenly she found herself looking into a room utterly different from any she had yet seen. Its low walls were of stone, its dusty windows shuttered; it contained nothing but a chair. And in that chair sat what appeared to be the life-size image of the smiling lovely creature she had seen in the portrait – eyes shut, cheeks a faint rose, hair still shimmering with gold, the hands laid idly in her lap, the fingers of one of them clutching what seemed to be the dried-up fragments of a bunch of roses. What there was to alarm her in this harmless image she could not tell; but she gazed awhile at it in horror, closed-to the door and ran off as if pursued by a nightmare, down one corridor and up another, to find herself at last by good fortune once more in the room where she had had her meal. It seemed, as she stood there, her hand upon her breast, as if she would never again recover her breath. She was no longer nervous; no longer merely timid: she was afraid. "If only, if only I had never come to this house!" was her one terrified thought.

She discovered with relief on re-entering Miss Cheyney's

presence that her godmother was still asleep. Alice could see awhile without being seen.

Now one of her mother's brothers – one of Alice's uncles, that is – was an old bachelor who delighted in birthday gifts. Alice had therefore been richer in dolls than most children: wooden, wax, china, Dutch, French, Russian, and even one from the Andaman Islands. But no single one of them had shown a face so utterly still and placid as that now leaning gently aside in its lace and silver cap and mantle. There was no expression whatever on its features. No faintest smile; no shadow of a frown. And yet the tiny wrinkles all over it, crooking down even from the brows over the eyelids, gave it the appearance of an exquisitely figured map.

And Alice was still surveying it as closely as some old treasure-hunter might the chart of his secret island, when the minute eyes reopened and her godmother was instantly awake and intent.

"Ah," whispered she, "I have myself been on a long journey, but I heard you calling. What happens, I wonder," and the tones sank lower, "what happens when one has ventured on too far to hear any such rumours? Answer me that, eh? But no matter. There is a more important question first. Tell me now, if you please, what you think of my house."

Alice moistened her lips. "That, great-grandmamma," she managed to reply at last, "that would take *ages*. It is marvellous: but oh, so very still."

"What should there be to disturb it?" asked the old lady.

Alice shook her head.

"Tell me," and her voice tinkled across the air with a peculiar little tang, "would you like this house for your own?"

"This house – for my own?" breathed the young girl.

"Ay, for your own, and for always – humanly speaking."

"I don't quite understand," said Alice.

The little head leaned sidelong like an inquisitive bird's.

"Naturally, my child. You *cannot* until I have gone a little further. The gift I am now offering you is one that few human beings in this world conceive to be possible. It is not merely this house, my child, with all that it contains – much as that may be. It is life. My father, you must understand, was a traveller; and in days when danger was a man's constant companion. In this very room on his return from a many years' journey, he told me as a girl of a dismal mountainous region of snow and ice and precipices that lies *there* – West of China, I believe. It was from hence that he brought back his secret. It was one that for grievous and tragical reasons he could not follow himself. And I, my child, was his only choice. You will realise there may come a day when the wish to live on may have somewhat dimmed in my mind. I confess to feeling a little weariness at times. But before I go, it is my privilege – my obligation – to confer the secret on another. Look at me!" The voice rose a little; it was as though a wren had uttered its shrill song in the low resounding room. "I am offering this inestimable benefit to *you*."

Alice sat straight as a dart in her chair, not venturing to turn her eyes aside even for a moment.

"The secret, great-grandmamma?"

"Ay," continued the old woman, closing her eyes, "you heard me aright. I will presently whisper it into your ear. Imagine my child, the wonder of infinite time! Imagine a life in such surroundings as these, far from all the follies and vexations of the world – and one fear – the most terrible of all fears – gone, or at any rate so remote as to be of no consequence. Imagine that, I say."

For an instant Alice's gaze wavered. Her eyes glanced swiftly towards the window where shone the swiftly changing colours of the sunset; where sang the wild birds, and Spring was fleeting on its way.

"Take your own time: and do not be afraid of me. I shall make few conditions. Only that you must vow silence, to breathe not one syllable of what I shall tell you – not even to your own mother. All else will be easy – comparatively easy. All else. You will come here and live with me. Rooms are prepared for you – books, music, horses to ride, servants to wait on you, all that you need. And in due season this house, this accumulation of things precious and old and beautiful, this wide park stretching for many more miles than you can see from my topmost windows, will be yours alone. You may pine for a while for old friends. It is an unhappy thing to say good-bye, as I have heard. But all fades, all goes. And in time you will not wish for company. Servants as aged as mine are not difficult to find; they are discreet, and have need to remain faithful. We shall have many a quiet talk together. I have much to tell you. I long, my dear child, to share memories with you that I have never breathed to a living soul. There are wings to this house into which you cannot have penetrated, simply because they are shut off by bolts and bars. They contain much to see: much to linger over; much to wonder at. Yes, and my dear child, in you I should live on – our two minds . . . two lives. Tell me now, what do you think of my proposal? And remember this: – Not even Solomon in all his glory could have conferred on you what I now offer."

The aged head was nodding – as if with fatigue. The cramped fingers fumbled aimlessly with the lace handkerchief, and Alice's poor wits were once more in a desperate confusion. The room swam dizzily before her eyes. She shut them a moment; endeavouring in vain to consider calmly what that remote unhuman voice had been saying to her. She might as well have struggled in sleep to shake off the veils and nets of a dream, the snares of a nightmare. One thing only was audible to her now, a bird singing in the garden and the sound of her shoe tapping on the floor. She listened – and came back.

"You mean," she whispered, "on and on and on – like you, great-grandmamma?"

The old lady made no reply.

"May I, do you think, then, if you would be so kind, may I have time to think it over?"

"Think what over?" said her godmother. "Are you supposing a child of your age can think over three complete centuries before a single moment of them has come into view?"

"No," said Alice, her courage returning a little, "I meant,

think over what you have said. It is so very difficult to realise what it means."

"It means," said the old lady, "an immeasurable sea, infinite space, an endless vista – of time. It means freedom from the cares and anxieties and follies that are the lot of the poor creatures in the world beyond – living out their few days in brutish stupidity. You are still young, but who knows? It means, my child, postponing a visit to a certain old friend of ours – whose name is Death."

She breathed the word as if in begrudged pleasure at its sound. Alice shuddered, and yet it gave her fresh resolution. She rose from her chair.

"I am young and stupid, I know, great-grandmamma; and I would do anything in the world not to – not to hurt your feelings. And of course, of course I know that most people have a very hard time and that most of us are not very sharp-witted. But you said *death*; and I think, if you will forgive my saying so, I would rather I should have to die when – just when, I mean, I *must* die. You see, it would be a very sorrowful thing for me if it came after my mother had – If, I mean, she cannot share the secret too? And even then . . . Why cannot we all share it? I do see, indeed I do, there is very little time in this world in which to grow wise. But when you think of the men who have—"

"You are here, my child," Miss Cheyney interrupted her, "to answer questions – not to ask them. I must not be fatigued. Then I should have no sleep. But surely you are old enough to know that there is not a human creature in a thousand, nay, not one in a hundred thousand, who has any hope of growing wise, not if he lived till Doomsday."

She edged forward an inch in her chair. "Suppose, my child, your refusal means that this secret will perish with – with *me*? Unless," the voice sank to a muttering, "unless *you* consent to share it? Eh, what then?"

Alice found her eyes fixed on the old lady like a bird's on a serpent, and the only answer she could make was a violent shake of the head. "Oh," she cried, suddenly bursting into tears, "I simply can't tell you how grateful I am for all your kindness, and how miserable I seem to myself to be saying this. But please, Miss Cheyney, may I go now? I feel a dreadful thing might happen if I stay here a minute longer."

The old lady seemed to be struggling in her chair, as if in the effort to rise out of it; but her strength failed her. She lifted her claw-like mittened hand into the air.

"Begone at once, then," she whispered, "at once. Even my patience is limited. And when the day comes that will remind you of my kindness, may you wish you had . . . Oh, oh! . . . " The frail voice rose shrill as a gnat's, then ceased. At sound of it the old butler came hastening in at the further door; and Alice slipped out of the other . . .

Not until the house had vanished from sight behind the leaping branches of its forest-trees did she slacken her pace to recover her breath. She had run wildly on, not daring to pause or even glance over her shoulder, as if her guardian angel were at her heels, lending wings to her feet to save her from danger.

That evening she and her mother – seated in the cosy red-curtained coffee-room of the "Red Lion" – actually sipped together a brimming glass of the landlord's old Madeira. Alice had never before kept any secret from her mother. Yet though she was able to tell her most of what had happened that afternoon, she could not persuade herself to utter a syllable about the purpose which had prompted Miss Cheyney to send her so improbable an invitation. Not then, nor ever afterwards.

"Do you really mean, my own dearest," her mother repeated more than once, pressing her hand as they sat in the chill spring night under the old oil-lamp-post awaiting their train in the little country railway station; "do you mean she never gave you a single little keepsake; never offered you *anything* out of all those wonderful treasures in that dreadful old house?"

"She asked me, mother dear," said Alice, turning her face away towards the dark-mouthed tunnel through which they would soon be venturing – "she asked me if I would like ever to be as old as she was. And honestly, I said I would much prefer to stay just the silly green creature I am, so long as I can be with you."

It was an odd thing to do – if the station-master had been watching them – but, however odd, it is certainly true that at this moment mother and daughter turned and flung their arms about each other's necks and kissed each other in such a transport as if they had met again for the first time after an enormous journey.

Not that Alice had been quite accurate in saying that her godmother had made her no gift. For a day or two afterwards there came by post a package; and enwrapped in its folds of old Chinese paper Alice found the very portrait she had seen on the wall on that already seemingly far-off day – the drawing, I mean, made by a pupil of the famous Hans Holbein, depicting her great-great-great-great-great-great-great-great-grandmother in the year of grace 1564, when she was just turned seventeen.

The Shape of Things

RAY BRADBURY

He did not want to be the father of a small blue pyramid. Peter Horn hadn't planned it that way at all. Neither he nor his wife imagined that such a thing could happen to them. They had talked quietly for days about the birth of their coming child, they had eaten normal foods, slept a great deal, taken in a few shows, and, when it was time for her to fly in the helicopter to the hospital, he had laughed and kissed her.

"Honey, you'll be home in six hours," he said. "These new birth-mechanisms do everything but father the child for you."

She remembered an old-time song. "No, no, they can't take *that* away from me!" and sang it, and they laughed as the helicopter lifted them over the green way from country to city.

The doctor, a quiet gentleman named Wolcott, was very confident. Polly Ann, the wife, was made ready for the task ahead and the father was put, as usual, out in the waiting room where he could suck on cigarettes or take highballs from a convenient mixer. He was feeling pretty good. This was the first baby, but there was not a thing to worry about. Polly Ann was in good hands.

Dr Wolcott came into the waiting room an hour later. He looked like a man who has seen death. Peter Horn, on his third highball, did not move. His hand tightened on the glass and he whispered:

"She's dead."

"No," said Wolcott, quietly. "No, no, she's fine. It's the baby."

"The baby's dead, then."

"The baby's alive, too, but – drink the rest of that drink and come along after me. Something's happened."

Yes, indeed, something had happened. The "something" that had happened had brought the entire hospital out into the corridors. People were going and coming from one room to another. As Peter Horn was led through a hallway where attendants in white uniforms were standing around peering into each other's faces and whispering, he became quite sick. The entire thing had the air of a carnival, as if at any moment someone might step up upon a platform and cry:

"Hey, looky looky! The child of Peter Horn! Incredible!"

They entered a small clean room. There was a crowd in the room, looking down at a low table. There was something on the table.

A small blue pyramid.

"Why've you brought me here?" said Horn, turning to the doctor.

The small blue pyramid moved. It began to cry.

Peter Horn pushed forward and looked down wildly. He was very white and he was breathing rapidly. "You don't mean that's it?"

The doctor named Wolcott nodded.

The blue pyramid had six blue snake-like appendages and three eyes that blinked from the tips of projecting structures.

Horn didn't move.

"It weighs seven pounds, eight ounces," someone said.

Horn thought to himself, they're kidding me. This is some joke. Charlie Ruscoll is behind all this. He'll pop in a door any moment and cry "April Fool!" and everybody'll laugh. That's not my child. Oh, horrible! They're kidding me.

Horn stood there, and the sweat rolled down his face.

Dr Wolcott said, quietly, "We didn't dare show your wife. The shock. She mustn't be told about it – now."

"Get me away from here." Horn turned and his hands were opening and closing without purpose, his eyes were flickering.

Wolcott held his elbow, talking calmly. "This is your child. Understand that, Mr Horn."

"No. No, it's not." His mind wouldn't touch the thing. "It's a nightmare. Destroy the thing!"

"You can't kill a human being."

"Human?" Horn blinked tears. "That's not human! That's a crime against God!"

The doctor went on, quickly. "We've examined this – child – and we've decided that it is not a mutant, a result of gene destruction or rearrangement. It's not a freak. Nor is it sick. Please listen to everything I say to you."

Horn stared at the wall, his eyes wide and sick. He swayed. The doctor talked distantly, with assurance.

"The child was somehow affected by the birth pressure. There was a dimensional distructure caused by the simultaneous short-circuitings and malfunctionings of the new birth-mechs and the hypnosis machines. Well, anyway," the doctor ended lamely, "your baby was born into – another dimension."

Horn did not even nod. He stood there, waiting.

Dr Wolcott made it emphatic. "Your child is alive, well, and happy. It is lying there, on the table. But because it was born into another dimension it has a shape alien to us. Our eyes, adjusted to a three-dimensional concept, cannot recognise it as a baby. But it *is*. Underneath that camouflage, the strange pyramidal shape and appendages, it is *your* child."

Horn closed his mouth and shut his eyes and wanted to think. "Can I have a drink?" he asked.

"Certainly," said Wolcott. "Here." A drink was thrust into Horn's hands.

"Now, let me just sit down, sit down somewhere a moment." Horn sank wearily into a chair. It was his child, no matter what. He shuddered. No matter how horrible it looked, it was his first child.

At last he looked up and tried to see the doctor. "What'll we tell Polly?" His voice was hardly a whisper. It was tired.

"We'll work that out this morning, as soon as you feel up to it."

"What happens after that? Is there any way to – change it back?"

"We'll try. That is, if you give us permission to try. After all, it's your child. You can do anything with him you want to do."

"Him?" Horn laughed ironically, shutting his eyes. "How do you know it's a him?" He sank down into darkness. His ears roared.

Wolcott was visibly upset. "Why, we – that is – well, we don't know, for sure."

Horn drank more of his drink. "What if you *can't* change him back?"

"I realise what a shock it is to you, Mr Horn. If you can't bear to look upon the child, we'll be glad to raise him here, at the Institute, for you."

Horn thought it over. "Thanks. But he's still my kid. He still belongs to me and Polly. I'll raise him. I'll give him a normal home life. Try to learn to love him. Treat him right." His lips were numb, he couldn't think.

"You realise what a job you're taking on, Mr Horn? This child can't be allowed to have normal playmates, why, they'd pester it to death in no time. You know how children are. If you decide to raise the child at home, his life will be strictly regimented, he must *never* be seen by anyone. Is that clear?"

"Yeah. Yeah, it's clear. Doc. Doc, is he okay mentally?"

"Yes. We've tested his reactions. He's a fine healthy child as far as nervous response and such things go."

"I just wanted to be sure. Now, the only problem is Polly."

Wolcott frowned. "I confess that one has me stumped. You know it is pretty hard on a woman to hear that her child has been born dead. But *this*, telling a woman she's given birth to something not recognisable as human. It's not as clean as death. There's too much chance for shock. And yet I must tell her the truth. A doctor gets nowhere by lying to his patient."

Horn put his glass down. "I don't want to lose Polly, too.

I'd be prepared now, if you destroyed the child, to take it. But I don't want Polly killed by the shock of this whole thing."

"I think we may be able to change the child back. That's the point which makes me hesitate. If I thought the case was hopeless I'd make out a certificate of euthanasia immediately. But it's at least worth a chance."

Horn was very tired. He was shivering quietly, deeply. "All right, doctor. It needs food, milk and love until you can fix it up. It's had a raw deal so far, no reason for it to go on getting a raw deal. When will we tell Polly?"

"Tomorrow afternoon, when she wakes up."

Horn got up and walked to the table which was warmed by a soft illumination from overhead. The blue pyramid sat upon the table as Horn held out his hand.

"Hello, baby," said Horn.

The blue pyramid looked up at Horn with three bright blue eyes. It shifted a tiny blue tendril, touching Horn's fingers with it.

Horn shivered.

"Hello, baby."

The doctor produced a special feeding bottle.

"This is woman's milk. Here, baby."

Baby looked upwards though clearing mists. Baby saw the shapes moving over him and knew them to be friendly. Baby was new-born, but already alert, strangely alert. Baby was aware.

There were moving objects above and around Baby. Six cubes of a grey-white colour, bending down. Six cubes with hexagonal appendages and three eyes to each cube. Then there were two other cubes coming from a distance over a crystalline plateau. One of the cubes was white. It had three eyes, too. There was something about this White Cube that Baby liked. There was an attraction. Some relation. There was an odour to the White Cube that reminded Baby of itself.

Shrill sounds came from the six bending down grey-white

cubes. Sounds of curiosity and wonder. It was like a kind of piccolo music, all playing at once.

Now the two newly arrived cubes, the White Cube, and the Grey Cube, were whistling. After a while the White Cube extended one of its hexagonal appendages to touch Baby. Baby responded by putting out one of its tendrils from its pyramidal body. Baby liked the White Cube. Baby liked. Baby was hungry. Baby liked. Maybe the White Cube would give it food. . . .

The Grey Cube produced a pink globe for Baby. Baby was now to be fed. Good. Baby accepted food eagerly.

Food was good. All the grey-white cubes drifted away, leaving only the nice White Cube standing over Baby looking down and whistling over and over. Over and over.

They told Polly the next day. Not everything. Just enough. Just a hint. They told her the baby was not well, in a certain way. They talked slowly, and in ever tightening circles, in upon Polly. Then Dr Wolcott gave a long lecture on the birth-mechanisms, how they helped a woman in her labour, and how, this time, they short-circuited. There was another man of scientific means present and he gave her a dry little talk on dimensions, holding up his fingers, so! one, two, three and four. Still another man talked of energy and matter. Another spoke of underprivileged children.

Polly finally sat up in bed and said, "What's all the talk for? What's wrong with my baby that you should all be talking so long?"

Wolcott *told* her.

"Of course, you can wait a week and see it," he said. "Or you can sign over guardianship of the child to the Institute."

"There's only one thing I want to know," said Polly.

Dr Wolcott raised his brows.

"Did I *make* the child that way?" asked Polly.

"You most certainly did *not*!"

"The child isn't a monster, genetically?" asked Polly.

"The child was thrust into another continuum. Otherwise, it is perfectly normal."

Polly's tight, lined mouth relaxed. She said, simply, "Then, bring me my baby. I want to see him. Please. Now."

They brought the "child".

The Horns left the hospital the next day. Polly walked out on her own two good legs, with Peter Horn following her, looking at her in quiet amazement.

They did not have the baby with them. That would come later. Horn helped his wife into their helicopter and sat beside her. He lifted the ship, whirring, into the warm air.

"You're a wonder," he said.

"Am I?" she said, lighting a cigarette.

"You are. You didn't cry. You didn't do anything."

"He's not so bad, you know," she said. "Once you get to know him. I can even – hold him in my arms. He's warm and he cries and he even needs his triangular nappies." Here she laughed. He noticed a nervous tremor in the laugh, however. "No, I didn't cry, Pete, because that's my baby. Or he will be. He isn't dead, I thank God for that. He's – I don't know how to explain – still unborn. I like to think he hasn't been born yet. We're waiting for him to show up, I have confidence in Dr Wolcott. Haven't you?"

"You're right. You're right." He reached over and held her hand. "You know something? You're a peach."

"I can hold on," she said, sitting there looking ahead as the green country swung under them. "I can wait. As long as I know something good will happen. I won't let it hurt or shock me. The mind is a great thing. If it has some hope, then it's cushioned all around. I'll wait six months," she said. And she looked over the edge of the helicopter. "And then maybe I'll kill myself."

"Polly!"

She looked at him as if he'd just come in. "Pete, I'm sorry. But this sort of thing doesn't happen. Once it's over and the baby is finally 'born' I'll forget it so quick it'll never have occurred. But if the doctor can't help us, then a mind can't take it, a mind can only tell the body to climb out on a roof and jump."

"Things'll be all right," he said, holding to the guide-wheel. "They *have* to be."

She said nothing, but let the cigarette smoke blow out of her mouth in the pounding concussion of the helicopter fan.

Three weeks passed. Every day they flew in to the Institute to visit "Py". For that was the quiet calm name that Polly Horn gave to the blue pyramid that lay on the warm sleeping-table and blinked up at them. Dr Wolcott was careful to point out that the habits of the "child" were as normal as any others; so many hours' sleep, so many awake, so much attentiveness, so much boredom, so much food, so much elimination. Polly Horn listened, and her face softened and her eyes warmed.

At the end of the third week, Dr Wolcott said, "Feel up to taking him home now? You live in the country, don't you? All right, you have an enclosed patio, he can be out there in the sunlight, on occasion. He needs a mother's love. That's trite, but nevertheless true. He should be suckled. We have an arrangement where he's been fed by the new feed-mech; cooing voice, warmth, hands, and all." Dr Wolcott's voice was dry. "But still I feel you are familiar enough with him now to know he's a pretty healthy child. Are you game, Mrs Horn?"

"Yes. I'm game."

"Good. Bring him in every third day for a check-up. Here's his formula. We're working on several ideas now, Mrs Horn. We should have some results for you by the end of the year. I don't want to say anything definite, but I have reason to believe we'll pull that boy right out of the fourth dimension, like a rabbit out of a hat."

The doctor was mildly surprised and pleased when Polly Horn kissed him, then and there.

Pete Horn took the 'copter home over the smooth rolling greens of Griffith. From time to time he looked at the pyramid lying in Polly's arms. She was making cooing noises at it, it was replying in approximately the same way.

"I wonder," said Polly.

"What?"

"How do *we* look to it?" asked his wife.

"I asked Wolcott about that. He said we probably look funny to him, also. He's in one dimension, we're in another."

"You mean we don't look like men and women to him?"

"If we could see ourselves, no. But remember, the baby knows nothing of men or women. To the baby whatever shape we're in, we are natural. It's accustomed to seeing us shaped like cubes or squares or pyramids, as it sees us from its separate dimension. The baby's had no other experience, no other norm with which to compare what it sees. We *are* its norm. On the other hand, the baby seems weird to us because we compare it to our accustomed shapes and sizes."

"Yes, I see. I see."

Baby was conscious of movement. One White Cube held him in warm appendages. Another White Cube sat further over, within an oblong of purple. The oblong moved in the air over a vast bright plain of pyramids, hexagons, oblongs, pillars, bubbles and multi-coloured cubes.

One White Cube made a whistling noise. The other White Cube replied with a whistling. The White Cube that held him shifted about. Baby watched the two White Cubes, and watched the fleeing world outside the travelling bubble.

Baby felt – sleepy. Baby closed his eyes, settled his pyramidal youngness upon the lap of the White Cube, and made faint little noises. . . .

"He's asleep," said Polly Horn.

Summer came, Peter Horn himself was busy with his export-import business. But he made certain he was home every night. Polly was all right during the day, but, at night, when she had to be alone with the child, she got to smoking too much, and one night he found her passed out on the sofa, an empty sherry bottle on the table beside her. From then on, he took care of the child himself at nights. When it cried it made a weird whistling noise, like some jungle animal lost and wailing. It wasn't the sound of a baby.

Peter Horn had the nursery sound-proofed.

"So your wife won't hear your baby crying?" asked the workman.

"Yeah," said Peter Horn. "So she won't hear."

They had few visitors. They were afraid that by some accident or other someone might stumble on Py, dear sweet pyramidal little Py.

"What's that noise?" asked a visitor one evening, over his cocktail. "Sounds like some sort of bird. You didn't tell me you had an aviary, Peter?"

"Oh, yes," said Horn, going and closing the nursery door. "Have another drink. Let's get drunk, everybody."

It was like having a dog or a cat in the house. At least that's how Polly looked upon it. Pete Horn watched her and observed exactly how she talked and petted the small Py. It was Py this and Py that, but somehow with some reserve, and sometimes she would look around the room and touch herself, and her hands would clench, and she would look lost and afraid, as if she were waiting for someone to arrive.

In September, Polly reported to Pete: "He can say Daddy. Yes he can. Come on, Py. Say Daddy!"

She held the blue warm pyramid up.

"Wheelly," whistled the little warm blue pyramid.

"Daddy," repeated Polly.

"Wheelly!" whistled the pyramid.

"For heaven's sake, cut it out!" shouted Pete Horn. He took the child from her and put it in the nursery where it whistled over and over that name, that name, that name. Whistled, whistled. Horn came out and got himself a stiff drink. Polly was laughing quietly, bitterly.

"Isn't that terrific?" she said. "Even his *voice* is in the fourth dimension. I teach him to say Daddy and it comes out Wheelly. He says Daddy, but it sounds like Wheelly to *us*!" She looked at her husband. "Won't it be nice when he learns to talk later? We'll give him Hamlet's soliloquy to memorise and he'll say it but it'll come out, 'Wheelly-roth-urll whee whistle wheet!' " She mashed out her cigarette. "The offspring of James Joyce! Aren't we lucky?" She got up. "Give me a drink."

"You've had enough," he said.

"Thanks, I'll help myself," she said and did.

October, and then November, Py was learning to talk now. He whistled and squealed and made a bell-like tone when he was hungry. Dr Wolcott visited. "When his colour is a constant bright blue," said the doctor, "that means he's healthy. When the colour fades, dull – the child is feeling poorly. Remember that."

"Oh, yes, I will, I will," said Polly. "Robin's egg blue for health. Dull cobalt for illness."

"Young lady," said Wolcott. "You'd better take a couple of these pills and come see me tomorrow for a little chat. I don't like the way you're talking. Stick out your tongue. Ah-hmm. Give me your wrist. Pulse bad. Your eyes, now. Have you been drinking? Look at the stains on your fingers. Cut the cigarettes in half. I'll see you tomorrow."

"You don't give me much to go on," said Polly. "It's been almost a year now."

"My dear Mrs Horn, I don't want to excite you continually. When we have our mechs ready we'll let you know. We're working every day. There'll be an experiment soon. Take those pills now and shut that nice mouth." He chucked Py under the "chin". "Good healthy baby, by gravy! Twenty pounds if he's an *ounce*!"

Baby was conscious of the goings and comings of the Two White Cubes. The two nice White Cubes who were with him during all of his waking hours. There was another Cube, a grey one, who visited on certain days. But mostly it was the two White Cubes who cared for and loved him. He looked up at the one warm, rounder, softer White Cube and made the low warbling soft sound of contentment. The White Cube fed him. He was content. He grew. All was familiar and good.

The New Year arrived.

Peter Horn carted home large plates of specially poured blue and grey polarised glass, secretly. Through these, he peered at his "child". Nothing doing. The pyramid remained a pyramid, no matter if he viewed it through X-ray or yellow cellophane. The barrier was unbreakable. Horn returned quietly to his drinking.

The big thing happened early in February. Horn, arriving home in his helicopter, was appalled to see a crowd of neighbours gathered on the lawn of his home. Some of them were sitting, others were standing, still others were moving away, with frightened expressions on their faces.

Polly was walking the "child" in the yard.

Polly was quite drunk. She held the small blue pyramid by the hand and walked him up and down. She did not see the helicopter land, nor did she pay much attention as Horn came running up.

One of the neighbours turned. "Oh, Mr Horn, it's the cutest thing. Where'd you *find* it?"

One of the others cried, "Hey, you're quite the traveller, Horn. Pick it up in South America?"

Polly held the pyramid up. "Say Daddy!" she cried, trying to focus on her husband.

"Wheelly!" cried the pyramid.

"Polly!" shouted Peter Horn, and strode forward.

"He's friendly as a dog or a cat," said Polly staggering along, taking the child with her. She laughed at the neighbours. "Oh, no, he's not dangerous. He looks dangerous, yes, but he's not. He's friendly as a baby. My husband brought him from Afghanistan the other day. Has anybody got a drink?"

The neighbours began to move off when Peter Horn glared at them.

"Come back!" Polly waved at them. "Come back! Don't you want to see my baby? *Don't* you? Yes, he's my *child*, my very *own*! Isn't he simply beautiful?"

He slapped her face.

"My baby," she said, brokenly.

He slapped her again and again until she quit saying it and collapsed. He picked her up and took her into the house. Then he came out and took Py in and then he sat down and phoned the Institute.

"Dr Wolcott. This is Horn. You'd better get your stuff ready for the experiment. It's tonight or not at all."

There was a hesitation. Finally Wolcott sighed. "All right. Bring your wife and the child. We'll try to have things in shape."

They hung up.

Horn sat there studying the pyramid.

"The neighbours thought he was the cutest pet," said his wife, lying on the couch, her eyes shut, her lips trembling. . . .

The Institute hall smelled clean, neat, sterile. Dr Wolcott walked along it, followed by Peter Horn and his wife Polly, who was holding Py in her arms. They turned in at a doorway and stood in a large room. In the centre of the room were two tables with large black hoods suspended over them.

Behind the tables were a number of machines with dials and levers on them. There was the faintest perceptible hum in the room. Peter Horn looked at Polly for a moment.

Wolcott gave her a glass of liquid. "Drink this." She drank it. "Now. Sit down." They both sat. The doctor put his hands together and looked at them for a moment.

"I want to tell you what I've been doing in the last few months," he said. "I've tried to bring the baby out of the dimension, fourth, fifth, or sixth, that it is in. I haven't said much to you about it, but every time you left the baby for a check-up we worked on the problem. Now, do not get excited, but, I think we have found a way out of our problem."

Polly looked up quickly, her eyes lighting. "What!"

"Now, now, wait a moment," Wolcott cautioned her. "I have a solution, but it has nothing to do with bringing the baby out of the dimension in which *it* exists."

Polly sank back. Horn simply watched the doctor carefully for anything he might say. Wolcott leaned forward.

"I can't bring Py out, but I can put you people *in*. That's it." He spread his hands.

Horn looked at the machine in the corner. "You mean you can send *us* into Py's dimension?"

"If you want to go badly enough."

"I don't know," said Horn. "There'll have to be more explained. We'll have to know what we're getting into."

Polly said nothing. She held Py quietly and looked at him.

Dr Wolcott explained. "We know what series of accidents, mechanical and electrical, forced Pye into his present state. We can reproduce those accidents and stresses. But bringing him *back* is something else. It might take a million trials and failures before we got the combination. The combination that jammed him into another space was an accident, but luckily we saw, observed and recorded it. There are no records for bringing one back. We have to work in the dark. Therefore, it will be easier to put *you* in the fourth dimension than to bring Py into ours."

Polly asked, simply and earnestly, "Will I see my baby as he really is, if I go into his dimension?"

Wolcott nodded.

Polly said, "Then, I want to go." She was smiling weakly.

"Hold on," said Peter Horn. "We've only been in this office five minutes and already you're promising away the rest of your life."

"I'll be with my real baby. I won't care."

"Dr Wolcott, what will it be like, in that dimension on the other side?"

"There will be no change that *you* will notice. You will both seem the same size and shape to one another. The pyramid will become a baby, however, you will have added an extra sense, you will be able to interpret what you see differently."

"But won't we turn into oblongs or pyramids ourselves? And won't you, doctor, look like some geometrical form instead of a human?"

"Does a blind man who sees for the first time give up his ability to hear or taste?"

"No."

"All right, then. Stop thinking in terms of subtraction.

Think in terms of addition. You're gaining something. You lose nothing. You know what a human looks like, which is an advantage Py doesn't have, looking out from his dimension. When you arrive "over there" you can see Dr Wolcott as *both* things, a geometrical abstract or a human, as you choose. It will probably make quite a philosopher out of you. There's one other thing, however."

"And that?"

"To everyone else in the world you, your wife and the child will look like *abstract forms*. The baby a triangle. Your wife an oblong perhaps. Yourself a hexagonal solid. The *world* will be shocked, not you."

"We'll be freaks."

"You'll be freaks," said Wolcott. "But you won't know it. You'll have to lead a secluded life."

"Until you find a way to bring all three of us out together."

"That's right. Until then. It may be ten years, twenty. I won't recommend it to you, you may both develop psychoses as a result of feeling apart, different. If there's anything paranoid in you, it'll come out. It's up to you, naturally."

Peter Horn looked at his wife, she looked back gravely.

"We'll go," said Peter Horn.

"Into Py's dimension?" said Wolcott.

"Into Py's dimension," said Peter Horn, quietly.

They stood up from their chairs. "We'll lose no other sense, you're certain, doctor? Hearing or talking. Will you be able to understand us when we talk to you? Py's talk is incomprehensible, just whistles."

"Py talks that way because that's what he thinks we sound like when our talk comes through the dimensions to him. He imitates the sound. When you are over there and talk to me, you'll be talking perfect English, because you know *how*. Dimensions have to do with senses and time and knowledge. Don't worry about that."

"And what about Py? When we come into his strata of existence. Will he see us as humans, immediately, and won't that be a shock to him? Won't it be dangerous?"

"He's awfully young. Things haven't got too set for him. There'll be a slight shock, but your odours will be the same, and your voices will have the same timbre and pitch and you'll be just as warm and loving, which is most important of all. You'll get on with him well."

Horn scratched his head slowly. "This seems such a long way around to where we want to go." He sighed. "I wish we could have another kid and forget all about this one."

"This baby is the one that counts. I dare say Polly here wouldn't want any other, would you, Polly? Besides, she *can't* have another. I didn't say anything before, but her first was her *last.* It's either *this* baby or none at all."

"This baby, *this* baby," said Polly.

Wolcott gave Peter Horn a meaningful look. Horn interpreted it correctly. This baby or no more Polly ever again. This baby or Polly would be in a quiet room somewhere staring into space for the rest of her life, quite insane. Polly took this whole thing as a personal failure of her own. Somehow she supposed *she* herself had forced the child into an alien dimension. She lived only to make right that wrong, to lose the sense of failure, fear and guilt. It had to be Py. It just simply *had* to be Py. You couldn't reason Polly out of it. There was the evidence, the pyramid, to prove her guilt. It had to be Py.

They walked towards the machine together. "I guess I can take it, if she can," said Horn, taking her hand. "I've worked hard for a good many years now, it might be fun retiring and being an abstract for a change."

"I envy you the journey, to be honest with you," said Wolcott, making adjustments on the large dark machine. "I don't mind telling you that as a result of your being "over there" you may very well write a volume of philosophy that will set Dewey, Bergson, Hegel or any of the others on their ears. I might 'come over' to visit you one day."

"You'll be welcome. What do we need for the trip?"

"Nothing. Just lie on these tables and be still."

A humming filled the room. A sound of power and energy and warmth.

They lay on the tables, holding hands, Polly and Peter Horn. A double black hood came down over them. They were both in darkness. From somewhere far off in the hospital, a voice-clock sang, "Tick tock, seven o'clock. Tick tock, seven o'clock . . . " fading away in a little soft gong.

The low humming grew louder. The machine glittered with hidden, shifting, compressed power.

"Will we be killed, is there any chance of that?" cried Peter Horn.

"No, none!"

The power screamed! The very atoms of the room divided against each other, into alien and enemy camps. The two sides fought for supremacy. Horn opened his mouth to shout as he felt his insides becoming pyramidal, oblong with the terrific electrical wrestlings in the air. He felt a pulling, sucking, demanding power clawing at his body. Wolcott was on the right track, by heavens! The power yearned and nuzzled and pressed through the room. The dimensions of the black hood over his body were stretched, pulled into wild planes of incomprehension. Sweat, pouring down Horn's face, seemed more than sweat, it seemed a dimensional essence!

He felt his body webbed into a dimensional vortex, wrenched, flung, jabbed, suddenly caught and heated so it seemed to melt like running wax.

A clicking sliding noise.

Horn thought swiftly, but calmly. How will it be in the future with Polly and I and Py at home and people coming over for a cocktail party? How will it be?

Suddenly he knew how it would be and the thought of it filled him with a great awe and a sense of credulous faith and time. They would live in the same white house on the same quiet, green hill, with a high fence around it to keep out the merely curious. And Dr Wolcott would come to visit, park his beetle in the yard below, come up the steps and at the door would be a tall slim White Rectangle to meet him with a dry martini in its snake-like hand.

And in an easy chair across the room would sit a Salt White

Oblong seated with a copy of Nietzsche open, reading, smoking a pipe. And on the floor would be Py, running about. And there would be talk and more friends would come in and the White Oblong and the White Rectangle would laugh and joke and offer little finger sandwiches and more drinks and it would be a good evening of talk and laughter.

That's how it would be.

Click.

The humming noise stopped.

The hood lifted from Horn.

It was all over.

They were in another dimension.

He heard Polly cry out. There was much light. Then he slipped from the table, stood blinking. Polly was running. She stooped and picked up something from the floor.

It was Peter Horn's son. A living, pink-faced, blue-eyed boy, lying in her arms, gasping and blinking and crying.

The pyramidal shape was gone. Polly was crying with happiness.

Peter Horn walked across the room, trembling, trying to smile himself, to hold on to Polly and the boy baby, both at the same time, and cry with them.

"Well!" said Wolcott, standing back. He did not move for a long while. He only watched the White Oblong and the White slim Rectangle holding the Blue Pyramid on the opposite side of the room. An assistant came in the door.

"Shhh," said Wolcott, hand to his lips. "They'll want to be alone awhile. Come along." He took the assistant by the arm and tiptoed across the room. The White Rectangle and the White Oblong didn't even look up when the door closed.

Time Travelling

From *The Time Machine*
H. G. WELLS

"I told some of you last Thursday of the principles of the Time Machine, and showed you the actual thing itself, incomplete in the workshop. There it is now, a little travel-worn, truly; and one of the ivory bars is cracked, and a brass rail bent; but the rest of it's sound enough. I expected to finish it on Friday; but on Friday, when the putting together was nearly done, I found that one of the nickel bars was exactly one inch too short, and this I had to get re-made; so that the thing was not complete until this morning. It was at ten o'clock today that the first of all Time Machines began its career. I gave it a last tap, tried all the screws again, put one more drop of oil on the quartz rod, and sat myself in the saddle. I suppose a suicide who holds a pistol to his skull feels much the same wonder at what will come next as I felt then. I took the starting lever in one hand and the stopping one in the other, pressed the first, and almost immediately the second. I seemed to reel; I felt a nightmare sensation of falling; and, looking round, I saw the laboratory exactly as before. Had anything happened? For a moment I suspected that my intellect had tricked me. Then I noted the clock. A moment before, as it seemed, it had stood at a minute or so past ten; now it was nearly half-past three!

"I drew a breath, set my teeth, gripped the starting lever with both hands, and went off with a thud. The laboratory got hazy and went dark. Mrs Watchett came in, and walked, apparently without seeing me, towards the garden door. I suppose it took her a minute or so to traverse the place, but to me she seemed to shoot across the room like a rocket. I pressed the lever over to its extreme position. The night came like the turning out of a lamp, and in another moment came tomorrow. The laboratory grew faint and hazy, then fainter and ever fainter. Tomorrow night came black, then day again, night again, day again, faster and faster still. An eddying murmur filled my ears, and a strange, dumb confusedness descended on my mind.

"I am afraid I cannot convey the peculiar sensations of time travelling. They are excessively unpleasant. There is a feeling exactly like that one has upon a switchback – of a helpless headlong motion! I felt the same horrible anticipation, too, of an imminent smash. As I put on pace, night followed day like the flapping of a black wing. The dim suggestion of the laboratory seemed presently to fall away from me, and I saw the sun hopping swiftly across the sky, leaping it every minute, and every minute marking a day. I supposed the laboratory had been destroyed and I had come into the open air. I had a dim impression of scaffolding, but I was already going too fast to be conscious of any moving things. The slowest snail that ever crawled dashed by too fast for me. The twinkling succession of darkness and light was excessively painful to the eye. Then, in the intermittent darknesses, I saw the moon spinning swiftly through her quarters from new to full, and had a faint glimpse of the circling stars. Presently, as I went on, still gaining velocity, the palpitation of night and day merged into one continuous greyness; the sky took on a wonderful deepness of blue, a splendid luminous colour like that of early twilight; the jerking sun became a streak of fire, a brilliant arch, in space, the moon a fainter fluctuating band; and I could see nothing of the stars, save now and then a brighter circle flickering in the blue.

"The landscape was misty and vague. I was still on the hill-side upon which this house now stands, and the shoulder rose above me grey and dim. I saw trees growing and changing like puffs of vapour, now brown, now green: they grew, spread, shivered, and passed away. I saw huge buildings rise up faint and fair, and pass like dreams. The whole surface of the earth seemed changed – melting and flowing under my eyes. The little hands upon the dials that registered my speed raced round faster and faster. Presently I noted that the sun-belt swayed up and down, from solstice to solstice, in a minute or less, and that, consequently, my pace was over a year a minute; and minute by minute the white snow flashed across the world, and vanished, and was followed by the bright, brief green of spring.

"The unpleasant sensations of the start were less poignant now. They merged at last into a kind of hysterical exhilaration. I remarked, indeed, a clumsy swaying of the machine, for which I was unable to account. But my mind was too confused to attend to it, so with a kind of madness growing upon me, I flung myself into futurity. At first I scarce thought of stopping, scarce thought of anything but these new sensations. But presently a fresh series of impressions grew up in my mind – a certain curiosity and therewith a certain dread – until at last they took complete possession of me. What strange developments of humanity, what wonderful advances upon our rudimentary civilisation, I thought, might not appear when I came to look nearly into the dim elusive world that raced and fluctuated before my eyes! I saw great and splendid architecture rising about me, more massive than any buildings of our own time, and yet, as it seemed, built of glimmer and mist. I saw a richer green flow up the hill-side, and remain there without any wintry intermission. Even through the veil of my confusion the earth seemed very fair. And so my mind came round to the business of stopping.

"The peculiar risk lay in the possibility of my finding some substance in the space which I, or the machine, occupied. So long as I travelled at a high velocity through time, this scarcely mattered: I was, so to speak, attenuated – was slipping like a vapour through the interstices of intervening substances! But to come to a stop involved the jamming of myself, molecule by molecule, into whatever lay in my way: meant bringing my atoms into such intimate contact with those of the obstacle that a profound chemical reaction – possibly a far-reaching explosion – would result, and blow myself and my apparatus out of all possible dimensions – into the Unknown. This possibility had occurred to me again and again while I was making the machine; but then I had cheerfully accepted it as an unavoidable risk – one of the risks a man has got to take! Now the risk was inevitable, I no longer saw it in the same cheerful light. The fact is that, insensibly, the absolute strangeness of everything, the sickly jarring and swaying of the machine, above all, the feeling of prolonged falling, had absolutely upset my nerve. I told myself that I could never stop, and with a gust of petulance I resolved to stop forthwith. Like an impatient fool, I lugged over the lever, and incontinently the thing went reeling over, and I was flung headlong through the air.

"There was the sound of a clap of thunder in my ears. I may have been stunned for a moment. A pitiless hail was hissing round me, and I was sitting on soft turf in front of the overset machine. Everything still seemed grey, but presently I remarked that the confusion in my ears was gone. I looked round me. I was on what seemed to be a little lawn in a garden, surrounded by rhododendron bushes, and I noticed that their mauve and purple blossoms were dropping in a shower under the beating of the hailstones. The rebounding, dancing hail hung in a little cloud over the machine, and drove along the ground like smoke. In a moment I was wet to the skin. 'Fine hospitality,' said I, 'to a man who has travelled innumerable years to see you.'

"Presently I thought what a fool I was to get wet. I stood up and looked round me. A colossal figure, carved apparently in some white stone, loomed indistinctly beyond the rhododendrons through the hazy downpour. But all else of the world was invisible.

"My sensations would be hard to describe. As the columns of hail grew thinner, I saw the white figure more distinctly. It was very large, for a silver birch tree touched its shoulder. It was of white marble, in shape something like a winged sphinx, but the wings, instead of being carried vertically at the sides, were spread so that it seemed to hover. The pedestal, it appeared to me, was of bronze, and was thick with verdigris. It chanced that the face was towards me; the sightless eyes seemed to watch me; there was the faint shadow of a smile on the lips. It was greatly weather-worn, and that imparted an unpleasant suggestion of disease. I stood looking at it for a little space – half a minute, perhaps, or half an hour. It seemed to advance and to recede as the hail drove before it denser or thinner. At last I tore my eyes from it for a moment, and saw that the hail curtain had worn threadbare, and that the sky was lightening with the promise of the sun.

"I looked up again at the crouching white shape, and the full temerity of my voyage came suddenly upon me. What might appear when that hazy curtain was altogether withdrawn? What might not have happened to men? What if cruelty had grown into a common passion? What if in this interval the race had lost its manliness, and had developed into something inhuman, unsympathetic, and overwhelmingly powerful? I might seem some old-world savage animal, only the more dreadful and disgusting for our common likeness – a foul creature to be incontinently slain.

"Already I saw other vast shapes – huge buildings with intricate parapets and tall columns, with a wooded hillside dimly creeping in upon me through the lessening storm. I was seized with a panic fear. I turned frantically to the Time Machine, and strove hard to readjust it. As I did so the shafts of the sun smote through the thunderstorm. The grey downpour was swept aside and vanished like the trailing garments of a ghost. Above me, in the intense blue of the summer sky, some faint brown shreds of cloud whirled into nothingness. The great buildings about me stood out clear and distinct, shining with the wet of the thunderstorm, and picked out in white by the unmelted hailstones piled along their courses. I felt naked in a strange world. I felt as perhaps a bird may feel in the clear air, knowing the hawk wings above and will swoop. My fear grew to frenzy. I took a breathing space, set my teeth, and again grappled fiercely, wrist and knee, with the machine. It gave under my desperate onset and turned over. It struck my chin violently. One hand on the saddle, the other on the lever, I stood panting heavily in attitude to mount again.

"But with this recovery of a prompt retreat my courage recovered. I looked more curiously and less fearfully at this world of the remote future. In a circular opening, high up in the wall of the nearer house, I saw a group of figures clad in rich soft robes. They had seen me, and their faces were directed towards me.

"Then I heard voices approaching me. Coming through the bushes by the White Sphinx were the heads and shoulders of men running. One of these emerged in a pathway leading straight to the little lawn upon which I stood with my machine. He was a slight creature – perhaps four feet high – clad in a purple tunic, girdled at the waist with a leather belt. Sandals or buskins – I could not clearly distinguish which – were on his feet; his legs were bare to the knees, and his head was bare. Noticing that, I noticed for the first time how warm the air was.

"He struck me as being a very beautiful and graceful creature, but indescribably frail. His flushed face reminded me of the more beautiful kind of consumptive – that hectic beauty of which we used to hear so much. At the sight of him I suddenly regained confidence. I took my hands from the machine."

Blemish

JOHN CHRISTOPHER

Sunlight flooded through the open door of the forge, making friendly combat with the flames climbing up from the smith's fire. Joe Bredon, the smith, stood by his anvil hammering the glowing metal into shape. He heard no noise of approach under the ringing clash of his own work, but the visitor, standing in the doorway, blocked out some of the light and so announced himself. Joe Bredon looked up, shading his eyes. It was a young man – perhaps twenty-four or five – fantastically dressed in city clothes. He gave the horseshoe one last titanic pat and greeted the stranger.

"Mornin'. Anything we can do for you?"

The young man smiled with a practised ease that did not conceal his uneasiness.

"Guess it's the other way round. I want to help you. I represent Harkaway and Cummings, by the way. Biggest names in TV. Our new model, GK 34, is just what you want for your home entertainment. Full spectron colour, stereoscopic vision, five-thousand-mile range, two-foot screen . . . and very easy payments. And if you have an old H & C model we'll trade it in for you at 50 per cent of cost price. That's to show you that Harkaway and Cummings stand by their customers. Can I bring a set round to you for demonstration?"

Joe Bredon said laconically: "This your first trip, son?"

The young man faltered.

"Well, yes," he admitted. "I only finished Salesman College last month. What did I do wrong?"

Joe Bredon said: "We don't use TV here, son. Likewise we don't use magnet-sweepers nor frozen foods nor autogyros."

"Ah!" the young man said. "I see now. Some of our competitors have gypped you. Not every firm has the high ethical standards of Harkaway and Cummings. Now with our products you have a five-year guarantee of free servicing – can you ask for better than that?"

Joe Bredon said patiently: "You don't understand me, son. We don't want any contraptions from any firm. We just aren't interested."

The shocked surprise was excellently registered; the young man congratulated himself inwardly as he produced it.

"But if you don't have TV you don't know what you're missing! Girls, bands, comedians, thriller serials . . ." He glanced speculatively at the brawny smith, ". . . more girls. . . ."

Joe Bredon said: "You're wasting your time. Where you come from, son, that may not count for much. But you're wasting my time, too, and I have two horses to shoe and a sermon to prepare before I go to my dinner."

"So you're a preacher, too!" the young man said. "Why, only last Sunday the Ace Network ran a Church-in-the-Hills programme, right after the Follies. And next week there's the planet-wide hook-up of the arrival of the Galactic Ambassador. There's an inspiring scene for you. That will be something to write a sermon on."

Joe Bredon said: "I'll have to get Henry Tysing to paint us a new name-board. Seems clear you didn't see the old one. You don't know the name of this township, do you?"

"Well, no," the young man admitted, "I missed the name. But about these TV sets . . ."

"So I reckon I'd better tell you," Joe Bredon said. "This is Swan Upping."

The young man stopped at once.

"Swan Upping!" he exclaimed. "You mean, the . . ."

"Yes," Joe Bredon finished for him, ". . . the nuthouse. Mornin', son."

The Galactic Ambassador was a little staggering, at first sight. Life on the fourth planet of Sirius had found its dominant form amongst the octopods, and the Ambassador was rich in the possession of eight flourishing tentacles, on which his small body sat like an afterthought. The incongruity was enhanced by the slurred but correct and coherent English that issued from the small beaked mouth – the Ambassador had learned the language during the eight-week voyage from the Galactic capital. The World President, receiving him, was aware of the power vested in this strange creature, and had no desire to laugh.

The Ambassador said: "I think we must recapitulate the position, Mr President, so that you will fully understand our position and the purpose of my mission. In the first case your planet, of course, has been under Galactic surveillance for the past million years. Careful surveys were made at five-hundred-year intervals, without any interference, since interference, except when absolutely necessary, is abhorrent to the Galactic culture. Quite frankly we did not expect the fundamental problem of your suitability for inclusion in the Galactic culture to arise for several thousand years yet. However, our last survey, two years ago, had the shock of encountering an exploring spaceship half a light year outside the confines of your solar system. In five hundred years you had achieved a technological advance that is – you will be proud to learn – unparalleled in Galactic history. To advance in that time from animal transport to a gallant, if fool-hardy, attempt at interstellar travel . . . quite simply, we were amazed.

"As you will remember, our survey ship communicated with yours, gave it a brief outline of the nature and extent of Galactic culture, and sent it back to your planet with instructions that you should prepare for ambassadorial inspection – the essential and time-honoured preliminary to inclusion in

Galactic culture as a member state. I believe you were also informed that there have been cases in the past where inspection has revealed a civilisation so depraved that, as an act of kindness, it has been necessary to atomise the offending planet. I do not imagine that that will be so in this case, but it is necessary to warn you."

The Ambassador sprayed four tentacles forward in an expansive gesture that might have meant anything. The President nodded soberly.

"Well," the Ambassador said easily, "What shall we look at first?"

"This," said the World President with modest pride, "is the highest residential building on the planet. We house thirty thousand families in this apartment block alone. Fifty separate elevators, TV connections to every room, ten swimming pools, over a hundred built-in shops and a gyro landing base on the roof."

The Ambassador looked up at the block. It climbed effortlessly away into the withered blue sky.

"And all this area, of course," the President went on, "is under direct weather control. One hour's rainfall every twenty-four hours, between two and three a.m. So the fullest use can be made of the sun parlours laid out on every level. Though many people prefer to use the sunray lamps in their own apartment. They find them more convenient."

"A typical factory?" the Ambassador inquired.

"Absolutely," the President confirmed. "Plenty of air and space, and swing music from loud-speakers to provide a steady rhythmic background. Everything fool-proof. There hasn't been an accident here in over ten years."

"And the work?" said the Ambassador.

"All very easy. Simple mechanical jobs – machines do the hard work. And a statutory twenty-four-hour week with four weeks' holiday every year. No one lacks leisure."

"Leisure," the Ambassador said thoughtfully. "I should like to see some examples of leisure activity."

The autogyro hovered at fifty feet, the guarding police gyros drifting about them in a respectful circle. Beneath, on the oval of green turf, twenty-two opposing figures sweated and strained to gain a few inches with a leather ball. Around them, terraced up to the sky on all sides, more than two hundred thousand spectators surged and yelled in unison.

"Football," the President explained. "A very popular game."

Another crowd, barely fifty thousand this time, hushed and tense watching half a dozen superbly proportioned girls swooping and gliding in exquisite patterns, white flashing figures against black ice. The gentle blare of waltz music behind them. Spaced out at the periphery of a circle, they suddenly turned, leapt to seemingly certain collision at the centre, swerved and passed precisely, three between three. The exhaled sigh of the watching crowd was the gasp of a winded giant.

This crowd was more than a million. Spread out illimitably over the great plain, their faces were a white upturned sea, craning to watch the sky that arched over them. Through the air the coloured gyros flickered and danced, the long rod stretching from the nose of each plane to butt the vast bobbing ball towards the great suspended hoops at either end of the mile-long pitch. They weaved in dizzy convolutions and hundreds of thousands of necks slowly twisted to watch their flight. With a quick thrust the great ball was bobbing away towards one of the goals.

"Airball," the President said, "a new development. The ball's filled with a mixture of light and heavy gases; density just above that of air. Like thistledown, you might say. It's a very popular game."

. . .

"These are all hospitals?" the Ambassador asked. "You have a lot of sickness?"

"Practically none," the President affirmed. "But we include the nurseries with the hospitals, you know. When children are delivered the mother leaves them here. The parents visit very frequently, of course – as much as twice a week in some cases – but the babies are under the care of experts so that the parents are freed for other things. When the child is five it goes back to the parents and stays with them for three years before going away to boarding school."

"I see," said the Ambassador.

"The only real hospitalisation we now have is psychiatric," the President went on. "That big building in the centre. We do a lot of leucotomies – shearing the frontal lobe of the brain away to relieve depression. It makes them happy. Makes them a little irresponsible as well, of course, but we are past the stage of individual responsibility."

"Yes," said the Ambassador.

"And this is our main cultural centre," said the President. "Nine million cubic feet – isn't that something? Everything is co-ordinated from here on perfect democratic lines. We have a first-class sampling system which gives us a precision forecast of public taste. We know just what people like and we are able to give it to them. The result is that we never print any book now in a run of less than five million – and we never have more than ten thousand left unsold. That's accuracy to within 0.2 per cent!"

"The crematorium," the President said.

"For your dead?" the Ambassador asked.

"Yes. Cremation's universal now. All the big new residential blocks have special chutes built in – you can place a body in at the top and it's carried straight down to the crematorium and disposed of within ten minutes. All hygienic, no fuss."

"No rites?" asked the Ambassador. "I thought I saw on your TV recently . . ."

"Well, yes," said the President. "Some people find it quaint to take the ashes of their friends and relations along to one of the churches we keep as curiosities and sing a few hymns. It's like collecting stamps, you know. Individual kinks – not harmful."

They were back in the President's office. It had been a busy and rather nervous week, but the President felt pleased at a critical job well done. He leaned back, adjusting the dial of his oleofact to release an aura of pine trees round him – his favourite smell.

"I think I've shown you about everything, Your Excellency," he said. "If there are any questions . . . ?"

The Ambassador gestured ambiguously with two tentacles.

"No questions. I've almost made up my mind. There's only one thing. It is usual for an investigating Ambassador to choose some small district at random for closer inspection. Have you a World Gazetteer?"

The tentacles flipped carelessly through the great index, opened a page, delicately touched a line.

"This will do. Swan Upping. Will you take me to Swan Upping?"

The President smiled.

"You'll have to choose again, Your Excellency. That's a – uh – an asylum town. It's for anti-socials, crackpots."

The tentacle stayed firm in its place.

"Nevertheless, Mr President," said the Ambassador. "I should like to go there."

Outside Swan Upping there was a signboard: BUGGIES ONLY – POSITIVELY NO AUTOMOBILES. The President stopped the car.

"We can ignore that," he told the Ambassador, "for an occasion like this."

But the Ambassador was already getting out with a swift, flowing motion.

"No," he said, "we will not ignore it. We will go in on foot. Tell your police to wait here."

They walked into the village. Each house had clearly been built by hand and reflected the individual character of the builder; yet there was a strange sense of pattern overriding the minor variations. The President, trudging beside the Galactic Ambassador, let his eyes rove unhappily over the primitive, cobbled roadway, without either drains or sidewalks.

"It's amazing you should have picked on our one blemish," he said. "of course, we don't have many small townships, but I could have shown you hundreds with every device hygiene and planning can provide. And chance led you to this!" He paused in disgust as an infant of less than four toddled across their path from one front porch to an opposite one. "Primitives!"

They came through into the main street, and the Ambassador halted. The President pointed to the square-towered building dominating the rest.

"The church," he said. "They take that sort of thing seriously; natural primitive reaction, of course."

"And this?" asked the Ambassador.

A procession was coming down the street; black carriages pulled by sleek black animals. Their iron-shod hooves drew the bright fire of sparks from the cobbles beneath them.

"A funeral," the President said disinterestedly. "They actually *bury* their dead. The animals are what are known as horses – they use them here still for locomotion. In the real world they were extinct twenty years ago."

Opposite the church the procession drew up. Men in solemn black lifted the coffin from the hearse and carried it up stone steps into the churchyard, the mourners a slow eddy behind them. From the open door of the church organ notes began to peal.

"Our modern TV organs," the President remarked, "have ten times the range and volume."

In the churchyard the grave gaped, clay-yellow in the green grass. The following mourners began to sing, their voices rising clear and steady above the organ notes:

> *"Behold, all flesh is as the grass*
> *And all the goodliness of man*
> *Is as the flower of grass. . . ."*

When at last they stopped, the burly figure of Joe Bredon stepped forward. His voice was gentle and strong as he began to speak:

"Man that is born of woman . . ."

In the President's office for the third time the President waited confidently.

"And the decision, Your Excellency?" he asked.

"It has been reversed," pronounced the Ambassador. "When I saw the great apartment blocks where thirty thousand families were boxed in together, when I saw your factories where no man can take a pride in the work he does, when I saw the barren horror of your people's leisure with the million entertained by the antics of a tiny few, when I realised you have succeeded in destroying the sacred ties of the family and in your arrogance and overbearing pride have lost sight of the earth by which you live and the spirit by which all races are judged – when I saw these things there seemed only one decision: that this planet, sterile and withered as it is, should be atomised at once, for the Galaxy's good and for your own peace.

"But in one small township I have found spiritual life still strong, and by reason of that your planet is reprieved. You were on the right track once; you must retrace your steps to find it."

The President found words.

"And destroy our machines? We live by them – millions would starve. . . ."

"The machines are unimportant," said the Ambassador, "except in that your cleverness with them has led you to the pride and stupidity in which you now exist. We place no ban on machines – except spaceships. Until you have found humility and decency again you must not contaminate other worlds. That is our decision. In five hundred years a successor of mine will review it. Have you any questions to ask?"

"No," the President said slowly. "No, Your Excellency. No questions."

The Love Letter

JACK FINNEY

I've heard of secret drawers in old desks, of course; who hasn't? But the day I bought my desk I wasn't thinking of secret drawers and I know very well I didn't have any least premonition or feeling of mystery about it. I spotted it in the window of a secondhand store near my apartment, went in to look it over, and the proprietor told me where he got it. It came from one of the last of the big old mid-Victorian houses in Brooklyn; they were tearing it down over on Brock Place a few blocks away, and he'd bought the desk along with some other furniture, dishes, glassware, light fixtures, and so on. But it didn't stir my imagination particularly; I never wondered or cared who might have used it long ago. I bought it and lugged it home because it was cheap and because it was small; a legless little wall desk that I fastened to my living-room wall with heavy screws directly into the studding.

I'm twenty-four years old, tall and thin, and I live in Brooklyn to save money and work in Manhattan to make it. When you're twenty-four and a bachelor, you usually figure you'll be married before much longer and since they tell me that takes money I'm reasonably ambitious and bring work home from the office every once in a while. And maybe every couple weeks or so I write a letter to my folks in Florida. So I'd been needing a desk; there's no table in my phone-booth kitchenette, and I'd been trying to work at a wobbly end table I couldn't get my knees under.

I bought the desk one Saturday afternoon and spent an hour

or more fastening it to the wall. It was after six when I finished. I had a date that night, so I had time to stand and admire it for only a minute or so. It was made of heavy wood with a slant top like a kid's school desk and with the same sort of space underneath to put things into. But the back of it rose a good two feet above the desk top and was full of pigeonholes like an old-style roll-top desk. Underneath the pigeonholes was a row of three brass-knobbed little drawers. It was all pretty ornate; the drawer ends carved, some fancy scrollwork extending up over the back and out from the sides to help brace it against the wall. I dragged a chair up, sat down at the desk to try it for height, then got showered, shaved, and dressed, and went over to Manhattan to pick up my date.

I'm trying to be honest about what happened and I'm convinced that includes the way I felt when I got home around two or two-thirty that morning; I'm certain that what happened wouldn't have happened at all if I'd felt any other way. I'd had a good enough time that evening; we'd gone to an early movie that wasn't too bad, then had dinner, a drink or so and some dancing afterward. And the girl, Roberta Haig, is pretty nice – bright, pleasant, good-looking. But walking home from the subway, the Brooklyn streets quiet and deserted, it occurred to me that while I'd probably see her again I didn't really care whether I did or not. And I wondered, as I often had lately, whether there was something wrong with me, whether I'd ever meet a girl I desperately wanted to be with – the only way a man can get married, it seems to me.

So when I stepped into my apartment I knew I wasn't going to feel like sleep for a while. I was restless, half-irritated for no good reason, and I took off my coat and yanked down my tie, wondering whether I wanted a drink or some coffee. Then – I'd half forgotten about it – I saw the desk I'd bought that afternoon and I walked over and sat down at it, thoroughly examining it for the first time.

I lifted the top and stared down into the empty space underneath it. Lowering the top, I reached into one of the pigeonholes and my hand and shirt cuff came out streaked with old dust; the holes were a good foot deep. I pulled open one of the little brass-knobbed drawers and there was a shred of paper in one of its corners, nothing else. I pulled the drawer all the way out and studied its construction, turning it in my hands; it was a solidly made, beautifully mortised little thing. Then I pushed my hand into the drawer opening; it went in to about the middle of my hand before my finger tips touched the back; there was nothing in there.

For a few moments I just sat at the desk, thinking vaguely that I could write a letter to my folks. Then it suddenly occurred to me that the little drawer in my hand was only half a foot long while the pigeonholes just above the drawer extended a good foot back.

Shoving my hand into the opening again, exploring with my finger tips, I found a tiny grooved indentation and pulled out the secret drawer which lay in back of the first. For an instant I was excited at the glimpse of papers inside it. Then I felt a stab of disappointment as I saw what they were. There was a little sheaf of folded writing paper, plain white but yellowed with age at the edges, and the sheets were all blank. There were three or four blank envelopes to match, and underneath them a small, round, glass bottle of ink; and because it had been upside down, the cork remaining moist and tight in the bottle mouth, a good third of the ink had remained unevaporated still. Beside the bottle lay a plain, black wooden pen holder, the pen point reddish-black with old ink. There was nothing else in the drawer.

And then, putting the things back into the drawer, I felt the slight extra thickness of one blank envelope, saw that it was sealed, and I tipped it open to find the letter inside. The folded paper opened stiffly, the crease permanent with age, and even before I saw the date I knew this letter was old. The handwriting was obviously feminine, and beautifully clear – it's called Spencerian, isn't it? – the letters perfectly formed and very ornate, the capitals especially being a whirl of dainty curlicues. The ink was rust-black, the date at the top of the page was May 14, 1882, and reading it I saw that it was a love letter. It began:

Dearest! Papa, Mamma, Willy and Cook are long retired and to sleep. Now, the night far advanced, the house silent, I alone remain awake, at last free to speak to you as I choose. Yes, I am willing to say it! Heart of mine, I crave your bold glance, I long for the tender warmth of your look; I welcome your ardency, and prize it; for what else should these be taken but sweet tribute to me?

I smiled a little; it was hard to believe that people had once expressed themselves in elaborate phrasings of this kind, but they had. The letter continued, and I wondered why it had never been sent:

Dear one, do not ever change your ways. Never address me other than with what consideration my utterances should deserve. If I be foolish and whimsical, deride me sweetly if you will. But if I speak with seriousness, respond always with what care you deem my thoughts worthy. For, oh my beloved, I am sick to death of the indulgent smile and tolerant glance with which a woman's fancies are met. As I am repelled by the false gentleness and nicety of manner which too often ill conceal the wantonness they attempt to mask. I speak of the man I am to marry; if you could but save me from that!

But you cannot. You are everything I prize; warmly and honestly ardent, respectful in heart as well as in manner, true and loving. You are as I wish you to be – for you exist only in my mind. But figment though you are, and though I shall never see your like, you are more dear to me than he to whom I am betrothed.

I think of you constantly. I dream of you. I speak with you in my mind and heart; would you existed outside them! Sweetheart, good night; dream of me, too.

With all my love, I am,
your Helen

At the bottom of the page, as I'm sure she'd been taught in school, was written, "Miss Helen Elizabeth Worley, Brooklyn, New York", and as I stared down at it now I was no longer smiling at this cry from the heart in the middle of a long-ago night.

The night is a strange time when you're alone in it, the rest of your world asleep. If I'd found that letter in the daytime I'd have smiled and shown it to a few friends, then forgotten it. But alone here now, a window partly open, a cool late-at-night freshness stirring the quiet air, it was impossible to think of the girl who had written this letter as a very old lady or maybe long since dead. As I read her words, she seemed real and alive to me, sitting, or so I pictured her, pen in hand at this desk in a long, white, old-fashioned dress, her young hair piled on top of her head, in the dead of a night like this, here in Brooklyn almost in sight of where I now sat. And my heart went out to her as I stared down at her secret hopeless appeal against the world and time she lived in.

I am trying to explain why I answered that letter. There in the silence of a timeless spring night it seemed natural enough to uncork that old bottle, pick up the pen beside it, and then, spreading a sheet of yellowing old notepaper on the desk top, to begin to write. I felt that I was communicating with a still-living young woman when I wrote:

Helen: I have just read the letter in the secret drawer of your desk and I wish I knew how I could possibly help you. I can't tell what you might think of me if there were a way I could reach you. But you are someone I am certain I would like to know. I hope you are beautiful but you needn't be; you're a girl I could like, and maybe ardently, and if I did, I promise you I'd be true and loving. Do the best you can, Helen Elizabeth Worley, in the time and place you are; I can't reach you or help you. But I'll think of you. And maybe I'll dream of you, too.

Yours,
Jake Belknap

I was grinning a little sheepishly as I signed my name, knowing I'd read through what I'd written, then crumple the old sheet and throw it away. But I was glad I'd written it and I didn't throw it away. Still caught in the feeling of the warm, silent night, it suddenly seemed to me that throwing my letter away would turn the writing of it into a meaningless and foolish thing, though maybe what I did seems more foolish still. I folded the paper, put it into one of the envelopes and sealed it. Then I dipped the pen into the old ink, and wrote "Miss Helen Worley" on the face of the envelope.

I suppose this can't be explained. You'd have to have been where I was and felt as I did to understand it, but I wanted to mail that letter. I simply quit examining my feelings and quit trying to be rational; I was suddenly determined to complete what I'd begun, just as far as I was able to go.

My parents sold their old home in New Jersey when my father retired two years ago, and now they live in Florida and enjoy it. And when my mother cleared out the old house I grew up in, she packed up and mailed me a huge package of useless things I was glad to have. There were class photographs dating from grammar school through college, old books I'd read as a kid, Boy Scout pins – a mass of junk of that sort, including a stamp collection I'd had in grade school. Now I found these things on my hall-closet shelf in the box they'd come in, and I found my old stamp album.

It's funny how things can stick in your mind over the years; standing at the open closet door I turned the pages of that beat-up old album directly to the stamps I remembered buying from another kid with seventy-five cents I'd earned cutting grass. There they lay, lightly fastened to the page with a little gummed-paper hinge – a pair of two, mint condition two-cent United States stamps, issued in 1869. Standing in the hallway looking down at them I once again got something of the thrill I'd had as a kid when I acquired them. It's a handsome stamp, square in shape, with an ornate border and a tiny engraving in the centre, a rider on a galloping post horse. For all I knew they might have been worth a fair amount of money by now, especially an unseparated pair of two stamps. But back at the desk I pulled one of them loose, tearing carefully through the perforation, licked the back and fastened it to the faintly yellowing old envelope.

I'd thought no further than that; by now, I suppose, I was in a kind of trance. I shoved the old ink bottle and pen into a hip pocket, picked up my letter, and walked out of my apartment.

Brock Place, three blocks away, was deserted when I reached it; the parked cars motionless at the curbs, the high, late moonlight softening the lines of the big concrete supermarket at the corner. Then, as I walked on, my letter in my hand, there stood the old house just past a little shoe-repair shop. It stood far back from the broken cast-iron fence in the centre of its weed-grown lot, black-etched in the moonlight, and I stopped on the walk and stood staring up at it.

The high-windowed old roof was gone, the interior nearly gutted, the yard strewn with splintered boards and great chunks of torn plaster. The windows and doors were all removed, the openings hollow in the clear wash of light. But the high old walls, last of all to go, still stood tall and dignified in their old-fashioned strength and outmoded charm.

I walked through the opening where a gate had once hung, up the cracked and weed-grown brick pavement toward the wide old porch. And there on one of the ornate fluted posts I saw the house number deeply and elaborately carved into the old wood. At the wide flat porch rail leading down to the walk I brought out my envelope; 972 I printed under the name of the girl who had once lived here, Brock Place, Brooklyn, New York. Then I turned toward the street again, my envelope in my hand.

There was a mailbox at the next corner and I stopped beside it. But to drop this letter into that box, knowing in advance that it could go only to the dead-letter office, would again, I couldn't help feeling, turn the writing of it into an empty meaningless act; and after a moment I walked on past the box, crossed the street and turned right, knowing exactly where I was going.

I walked four blocks through the night passing a hack stand with a single cab, its driver asleep with his arms and head cradled on the wheel; passing a night watchman sitting on a standpipe protruding from the building wall smoking a pipe –

he nodded as I passed and I nodded in response. I turned left at the next corner, walked half a block more, then turned up onto the worn stone steps of the Wister postal substation.

It must easily be one of the oldest postal substations in the borough, built, I suppose, not much later than during the decade following the Civil War. And I can't imagine that the inside has changed much. The floor is marble, the ceiling high, the woodwork dark and carved. The outer lobby is open at all times as are post office lobbies everywhere, and as I pushed through the old swinging doors I saw that it was deserted. Somewhere behind the opaque windows a light burned dimly far in the rear of the post office and I had an impression of subdued activity back there. But the lobby was dim and silent and, as I walked across the worn stone of its floor, I knew I was seeing all around me precisely what Brooklynites had seen for no telling how many generations long dead.

The post office has always seemed an institution of mystery to me, an ancient, worn, but still functioning mechanism that is not operated but only tended by each succeeding generation of men to come along. It is a place where occasionally plainly addressed letters with clearly written return addresses go astray and are lost, to end up no one knows where and for reasons impossible to discover, as the postal employee from whom you inquire will tell you. Its air of mystery, for me, is made up of stories – well, you've read them, too, from time to time, the odd little stories in your newspaper. A letter bearing a postmark of 1906, written over half a century ago, is delivered today – simply because inexplicably it arrived at some post office along with the other mail with no explanation from anyone now alive. Sometimes it's a post card of greeting – from the Chicago World's Fair of 1893, maybe. And once, tragically, as I remember reading, it was an acceptance of a proposal of marriage offered in 1901 and received today, a lifetime too late, by the man who made it and who married someone else and is now a grandfather.

I pushed the worn brass plate open, dropped my letter into the silent blackness of the slot, and it disappeared forever with no sound. Then I turned and left to walk home with a feeling of fulfilment, of having done, at least, everything I possibly could in response to the silent cry for help I'd found in the secrecy of the old desk.

Next morning I felt the way almost anyone might. Standing at the bathroom mirror shaving, remembering what I'd done the night before, I grinned, feeling foolish but at the same time secretly pleased with myself. I was glad I'd written and solemnly mailed that letter and now I realised why I'd put no return address on the envelope. I didn't want it to come forlornly back to me with "no such person", or whatever the phrase is, stamped on the envelope. There'd once been such a girl and last night she still existed for me. And I didn't want to see my letter to her – rubber-stamped, scribbled on, and unopened – to prove that there no longer was.

I was busy all the next week. I work for a wholesale-grocery company; we got a big new account, a chain of supermarkets, and that meant extra work for everyone. More often than not I had my lunch at my desk in the office and worked several evenings besides. I had dates the two evenings I was free. On Friday afternoon I was at the main public library in Manhattan at Fifth Avenue and Forty-second copying statistics from half a dozen trade publications for a memorandum I'd been assigned to write over the weekend on the new account.

Late in the afternoon the man sitting beside me at the big reading-room table closed his book, stowed away his glasses, picked up his hat from the table and left. I sat back in my chair glancing at my watch. Then I looked over at the book he'd left on the table. It was a big one-volume pictorial history of New York put out by Columbia University, and I dragged it over, and began leafing through it.

I skimmed over the first sections on colonial and precolonial New York pretty quickly, but, when the old sketches and drawings began giving way to actual photographs, I turned the pages more slowly. I leafed past the first photos, taken around the mid-century, and then past those of the Civil War period. But when I reached the first photograph of the 1870s – it was a view of Fifth Avenue in 1871 – I began reading the captions under each one.

I knew it would be too much to hope to find a photograph of Brock Place, in Helen Worley's time especially, and of course I didn't. But I knew there'd surely be photographs taken in Brooklyn during the 1880s, and a few pages farther on I found what I'd hoped I might. In clear, sharp detail and beautifully reproduced lay a big half-page photograph of a street less than a quarter mile from Brock Place; and staring down at it, there in the library, I knew that Helen Worley must often have walked along this very sidewalk. VARNEY STREET, 1881, the caption said. A TYPICAL BROOKLYN RESIDENTIAL STREET OF THE PERIOD.

Varney Street today – I walk two blocks of it every night coming home from work – is a wasteland. I pass four cinder-packed used-car lots; a shabby concrete garage, the dead earth in front of it littered with rusting car parts and old tyres; and a half dozen or so nearly paintless boarding-houses, one with a soiled card in its window reading MASSAGE. It's a non-descript joyless street and it's impossible to believe that there has ever been a tree on its entire length.

But there has been. There in sharp black-and-white in the book on the table before me lay Varney Street, 1881, and from the wide grass-covered parkways between the cut-stone curb and sidewalks, the thick old long-gone trees rose high on both sides to meet, intertwine and roof the wide street with green. The photograph had been taken , apparently, from the street – it had been possible to do that in a day of occasional slow-trotting horses and buggies – and the camera was aimed at an angle to one side toward the sidewalk and the big houses beyond it, looking down the walk for several hundred feet.

The old walk, there in the foreground under the great trees, appeared to be at least six feet wide – spacious enough easily for a family to walk down it four or five abreast, as families did in those times walk together down the sidewalks under the trees. Beyond the walk, widely separated and set far back across the fine old lawns, rose the great houses, the ten-, twelve-, and fourteen-room family houses two or more storeys high and with attics above them for children to play in and discover the relics of childhoods before theirs. Their windows were tall and they were framed on the outside with ornamented wood. And in the solid construction of every one of those lost houses in that ancient photograph there had been left over the time, skill, money, and inclination to decorate their eaves with scrollwork; to finish a job with craftsmanship and pride. And time, too, to build huge wide porches on which families sat on summer evenings with palm-leaf fans.

Far down that lovely tree-sheltered street – out of focus and indistinct – walked the retreating figure of a long-skirted puff-sleeved woman, her summer parasol open at her back. Of the thousands of long-dead girls it might have been I knew this could not be Helen Worley. Yet it wasn't completely impossible, I told myself; this was a street, precisely as I saw it now down which she must often have walked; and I let myself think that, yes, this was she. Maybe I live in what is for me the wrong time and I was filled now with the most desperate yearning to be there on that peaceful street – to walk off past the edges of the scene on the printed page before me into the old and beautiful Brooklyn of long ago. And to draw near and overtake that bobbing parasol in the distance, and then turn and look into the face of the girl who held it.

I worked that evening at home, sitting at my desk, with a can of beer on the floor beside me, but once more Helen Elizabeth Worley was in my mind. I worked steadily all evening and it was around twelve-thirty when I finished – eleven handwritten pages which I'd get typed at the office on Monday. Then I opened the little centre desk drawer into which I'd put a supply of rubber bands and paper clips, took out a clip and fastened the pages together, and sat back in my chair, taking a swallow of beer. The little centre desk drawer stood half open as I'd left it and as my eye fell on it I realised that of course it, too, must have another secret drawer behind it.

I hadn't thought of that. It simply hadn't occurred to me the week before, in my interest and excitement over the letter I'd found behind the first drawer of the row; and I'd been too busy all week to think of it since. But now I set down my beer, pulled the centre drawer all the way out, reached behind it, and found the little groove in the smooth wood I touched. Then I brought out the second secret little drawer.

I'll tell you what I think, what I'm certain of, though I don't claim to be speaking scientifically; I don't think science has a thing to do with it. The night *is* a strange time; things *are* different then, as every human being knows. And I think this: Brooklyn has changed over seven decades; it is no longer the same place at all. But here and there, still, are little islands – isolated remnants of the way things once were. And the Wister postal substation is one of them; it hasn't really changed at all. And I think that at night – late at night, the world asleep, when the sounds of things as they are now are nearly silent and the sight of things as they are now is vague in the darkness – the boundary between here and then wavers. At certain moments and places it fades. I think that in the dimness of the old Wister post office in the dead of night, lifting my letter to Helen Worley toward the old brass door of the letter drop – I think that I stood on one side of that slot in the year 1962 and that I dropped my letter, properly stamped, written and addressed in the ink and on the very paper of Helen Worley's youth, into the Brooklyn of 1882 on the other side of that worn old slot.

I believe that – I'm not even interested in proving it – but I believe it. Because now from that second secret little drawer I brought out the paper I found in it, opened it, and in rust-black ink on yellowing old paper I read:

Please, oh, please – who are you? Where can I reach you? Your letter arrived today in the second morning post, and I have wandered the house and garden ever since in an agony of excitement. I cannot conceive how you saw my letter in its secret place, but since you did, perhaps you will see this one too. Oh, tell me your letter is no hoax or cruel joke! Willy, if it is you; if you have discovered my letter and think to deceive your sister with a prank, I pray you to tell me! But if it is not – if

I now address someone who has truly responded to my most secret hopes – do not longer keep me ignorant of who and where you are. For I, too – and I confess it willingly – long to see you! And I, too, feel and am most certain of it, that if I could know you I would love you. It is impossible for me to think otherwise.

I must hear from you again; I shall not rest until I do.

I remain, most sincerely,
Helen Elizabeth Worley

After a long time I opened the first little drawer of the old desk and took out the pen and ink I'd found there, and a sheet of the note paper.

For minutes then, the pen in my hand, I sat there in the night staring down at the empty paper on the desk top; finally I dipped the pen into the old ink and wrote:

Helen, my dear: I don't know how to say this so it will seem even comprehensible to you. But I do exist, here in Brooklyn, less than three blocks from where you now read this – in the year 1962. We are separated not by space but by the years which lie between us. Now I own the desk which you once had and at which you wrote the note I found in it. Helen, all I can tell you is that I answered that note, mailed it late at night at the old Wister station, and that somehow it reached you as I hope this will too. This is no hoax! Can you imagine anyone playing a joke that cruel? I live in a Brooklyn within sight of your house that you cannot imagine. It is a city whose streets are now crowded with wheeled vehicles propelled by engines. And it is a city extending far beyond the limits you know, with a population of millions, so crowded there is hardly room any longer for trees. From my window as I write I can see – across Brooklyn Bridge, which is hardly changed from the way you, too, can see it now – Manhattan Island, and rising from it are the lighted silhouettes of stone-and-steel buildings more than one thousand feet high.

You must believe me. I live, I exist eighty years after you

read this, and with the feeling that I have fallen in love with you.

I sat for some moments staring at the wall, trying to figure out how to explain something I was certain was true. Then I wrote:

Helen, there are three secret drawers in our desk. Into the first you put only the letter I found. You cannot now add something to that drawer and hope that it will reach me. For I have already opened that drawer and found only the letter you put there. Nothing else can now come down through the years to me in that drawer for you cannot alter what you have already done.

Into the second drawer you put the note which lies before me, which I found when I opened that drawer a few minutes ago. You put nothing else into it, and now that, too, cannot be changed.

But I haven't opened the third drawer, Helen. Not yet! It is the last way you can still reach me and the last time. I will mail this as I did before, then wait. In a week I will open the last drawer.

Jake Belknap

It was a long week. I worked, I kept busy daytimes, but at night I thought of hardly anything but the third secret drawer in my desk. I was terribly tempted to open it earlier, telling myself that whatever might lie in it had been put there decades before and must be there now, but I wasn't sure and I waited.

Then, late at night, a week to the hour after I'd mailed my second letter at the old Wister post office, I pulled out the third drawer, reached in and brought out the last little secret drawer which lay behind it. My hand was actually shaking and for a moment I couldn't bear to look directly – something lay in the drawer – and I turned my head away. Then I looked.

I'd expected a long letter, very long, of many pages, her last communication with me, and full of everything she wanted to say. But there was no letter at all. It was a photograph, about three inches square, a faded sepia in colour, mounted on heavy stiff cardboard, and with the photographer's name in tiny gold script down in the corner: *Brunner & Holland, Parisian Photography, Brooklyn, N.Y.*

The photograph showed the head and shoulders of a girl in a high-necked dark dress with a cameo brooch at the collar. Her dark hair was swept tightly back, covering the ears, in a style which no longer suits our ideas of beauty. But the stark severity of that dress and hair style couldn't spoil the beauty of the face that smiled out at me from that old photograph. It wasn't beautiful in any classic sense, I suppose. The brows were unplucked and somewhat heavier than we are used to. But it is the soft warm smile of her lips and her eyes – large and serene as she looks out at me over the years – that make Helen Elizabeth Worley a beautiful woman. Across the bottom of her photograph she had written, "I will never forget." And as I sat there at the old desk staring at what she had written, I understood that of course that was all there was to say – what else? – on this, the last time, as she knew, that she'd ever be able to reach me.

It wasn't the last time, though. There was one final way for Helen Worley to communicate with me over the years and it took me a long time, as it must have taken her, to realise it. Only a week ago, on my fourth day of searching, I finally found it. It was late in the evening and the sun was almost gone, when I found the old headstone among all the others stretching off in rows under the quiet trees. Then I read the inscription etched in the weathered old stone: HELEN ELIZABETH WORLEY – 1861–1934. Under this were the words, I NEVER FORGOT.

And neither will I.

Hallowe'en for Mr Faulkner

AUGUST DERLETH

There was simply no use going farther; so Guy Faulkner stood where he was, as helpless as if he were in the midst of a chartless sea. He was somewhere in London, in a sea of fog? Was it in Lambeth? And had he not heard the bells of St Clement's? He deplored his insistence on going out that afternoon in trace of some faint lead to supplement the work being done by Inigo Gunter, who was an expert in matters historical and genealogical, and whose report had been promised him this very day. A pox on his own impatience! Now there was no telling just when he would escape the fog.

He stood resolutely still. Sooner or later someone was bound to come along. If it were a bobby, he would be given good conduct to his hotel. If it were anyone at all familiar with the district, he might at least learn where he had wandered to. The fog swirled around him, growing ever more dense – not yellow, as he had been led to believe, but a kind of grey shot through with a glow rising as from distant lights which had no separate identity. He quelled his impatience; he had no alternative but to wait. He would have been almost as helpless in Chicago or New York, for all his familiarity with those cities, so thick was the fog.

Quite suddenly a dark shape loomed beside him.

"Pardon me," he said.

"Match, Guvnor?"

Faulkner took out his lighter. Fortunately, it lit at once. He held it up.

The fog played tricks on him. The face he looked into might have been his own. It bent to light a pipe, seemed to flatten, to dissolve – the fog again.

"I'm afraid I'm lost," said Faulkner.

"Come along," said the other, beginning to move away.

Faulkner followed. His companion walked with sureness and ease; he at least could find his way.

"I want to go to the Chelsea," he said.

But the other did not reply, and Faulkner had all he could do to keep up with him, trying to keep from falling over kerbs and colliding with lamp-posts. Should there not have been more light as they approached the hotel? he wondered. But abruptly his silent companion turned off the walk and mounted a few steps. Faulkner was conscious of a typical iron railing at either side. Coming up behind his guide, Faulkner lit his lighter again; the figure 16 gleamed on the heavy door. Then the door swung open upon a darkened hall, and immediately his guide was engulfed. Faulkner hesitated only a moment – anything was better than the oppressive fog. The door closed behind him, and another opened before upon a dimly lit room into which he had hardly stepped before he was aware of the strangeness of it – a room, as it were, of invaluable antique furnishings; it might have been lifted completely from a museum. He turned to his companion to ask – and found himself alone.

The door behind him closed. Down along one wall of the room was another door, beneath which showed a brighter light; and behind it rose the murmur of voices. Had his companion gone that way? But no, how could he? There had not been time. A sudden panic assailed Faulkner and he turned to go back the way he had come.

But even as his hand fell upon the knob, the door at the end of the room opened, a yellow glow spread into the room, and a hearty voice said to someone behind, "Here's Guy now! We were waiting for you."

Faulkner turned, surprised. A man masked with a domino. And in costume. Behind him, grouped about a table, were others, likewise costumed and masked. But, of course, the night was near to All Hallows and some people celebrated the time of masks throughout the week, into November; these were doubtless traditional masks, and known to him, perhaps, behind their masks. He hesitated but a moment more; the man before him held the door invitingly open, and his smile bade Faulkner welcome as no words need have done.

"You're late, Guy . . ."

"We thought you'd failed of coming . . ."

"What kept you?"

A chair was pushed forward for him.

Bewildered, he sat down. He was aware of a strange kind of apprehension within him, as if something ominous lay behind this mask of comradeship. He could not remember a voice, a face, a gesture. And yet, so familiar were these men, that he could not but wonder how he could have forgotten them. In a moment, certainly, their names would come to him; someone would mention them.

"I say, Wright, now Guy's here, we can get on with it."

Wright – John Wright, Faulkner said to himself. And that man talking was Tom Winter. And that, Robert Catesby. And the fourth, Tom Percy. And finally, Ambrose Rokewood. Faulkner could not recall where he had met them, yet their names were now certainly coming back to him. But the feeling of apprehension did not leave him.

He waited.

The bottles and glasses were pushed aside, and Catesby leaned over.

"The day's been chosen, you'll recollect, Guy."

"The fifth," said Winter.

One of them chuckled. "Was it not a clever thing to have chosen a night of this week for our last meeting? When so many are in costume, and the most improbable of all excites no question?"

"But for your own, Guy," said Wright. "A strange costume, indeed. And unmasked! How bold!"

"Ah, I am but an humble servant of Mr Percy," Faulkner said, and grinned.

But simultaneously he thought: Percy – but of course, he was employed by Percy. Had he not come over the sea from Flanders not long since? And spoken there with Stanley of Deventer? What nagged in his mind was a perplexity indeed. A broader ocean, a strange land, great cities . . .

"The powder's laid," continued Catesby.

"Aye, and the fuse is placed," said Percy. "He had good time in which to do these things from my house next door to Parliament House. A good and willing servant, indeed. Once this business is done with, I commend him to you. He will go to heights."

"One way or t'other," said Wright sourly. "High by his skill or by the scaffold if we're caught."

"Come, come, let us not speak of being caught," protested Catesby. "We've come a long way; we are on the threshold of success. Victory will be ours within the week, mark me."

"Who will light the fuse?" asked Rokewood. "I offer myself."

"Noble and generous Rokewood," said Catesby. "But this would scarce be fair to the others who are as eager to consummate this task. Shall we not draw for it?"

"Aye," said Wright.

And "Aye," said Percy.

Winter nodded, without saying anything, and Rokewood made no protest.

"It will be arranged before this night is done. Come now, let us look to plans to which we must adhere once the thing has been accomplished. Draw closer."

Catesby produced a map and spread it before them. Six heads circled it. Catesby's elegant fingers, dark against the white ruff at his wrist, descended to the map.

"The moment it is done, I will ride to my mother's house at Ashby St Legers. We shall, several of us, ride through Warwickshire to rally the country behind us. I myself will go straight to Digby and enlist his aid, by which time he will be ready, if I can tell him both James and Salisbury are dead."

"And what if they are not?" asked Rokewood.

"We dare not fail."

"There are thirty-six barrels of gunpowder under coal and faggots in the cellar. More than a ton of the stuff," said Percy.

"But, since it's been there so long – May, was it not? – what assurance have we that it has not got wet?"

"It was put in a dry place on purpose," said Percy, and turned to Faulkner. "Was it not, Guy?"

Faulkner nodded.

"And the Jesuits?"

"We have Garnet's blessing, at least. But Greenway and Gerard know our plan and have not spoken against it."

A doubt beset Faulkner. He closed his eyes. Instantly all this elaborate play was alien. He was Guy Faulkner of New York, in London in pursuing his genealogical studies. The year was 1953. But when he opened his eyes a moment later, he could have taken solemn oath that it was some other year. The candles flickered, and appurtenances of the house loomed grotesque in their age in the candlelight. The five masked men who stood about him, leaning over the map on the table, were impeccably dressed in the costumes of the seventeenth century's turn.

An elaborate hoax. Who could have been responsible for it? Or, for that matter, for his own words, spoken so glibly? Or was it a plot, indeed? Was it by some accident that he had stumbled upon an attempt to repeat history, to blow up Parliament? Apprehension spread through him again.

"Guy says little," said Wright suddenly.

"I am not man for words," Faulkner responded without hesitation.

"True," agreed Catesby. "Would that all others had to his credit Guy's deeds. We should not now be in doubt of the success of our plot. Where is Tresham?"

"None knows. Safe in his bed, most likely," said Percy.

"I said it was a mistake to invite Tresham to take part in

this," said Rokewood heavily. "Monteagle is his brother-in-law; can he contrive to keep him from Parliament and destruction with James and Salisbury?"

"He dare not."

"Who will say him nay? Was he not all eagerness and will at the beginning; but now that the thing is all but done, where is Tresham?" demanded Rokewood. "A peer's brother-in-law has no place among us."

"A man's a man not by any accident of blood," said Catesby.

"Nor of religion, then," said Percy.

"Agreed," said Catesby. "Or colour, age, or temper."

All this time Winter had said nothing. Now he put on the table six sticks he had been fashioning. All save one were of equal length; the one was shorter.

"How say we?" he asked.

"He who draws the short stick shall light the fuse," said Catesby.

There was an immediate chorus of agreement.

Catesby slipped on his gloves, so that he might not himself feel which was the short one among them, picked up the sticks, rolled them about a little, and held them out, stuck in his fist.

Percy drew first.

Then Rokewood. Since both had sticks of equal length, neither had drawn the short one.

Winter drew – a long stick.

Wright – another of similar length.

Catesby grinned sardonically, and held the two remaining sticks before Faulkner. "It lies between us, Guy. Fate would have it so."

Faulkner drew. He had the short stick.

Catesby opened his hand, let the remaining stick fall. "I congratulate you, Guy. None could better perform this task to free our great country from the oppressions of James and Salisbury."

Faulkner smiled. Uncertainty, apprehension, astonishment vied for revelation, but none showed on his features.

"You'll remember what was agreed upon," Catesby went on. "You'll get into the cellar in the night, and, as soon as the King has arrived, light the fuse and make your escape at once. Fly to join me at Ashby St Legers."

Rokewood came to his feet, a heavy man, dark of feature. He reached behind him for his cloak. "The thing's as good as done. I bid you goodnight, gentlemen. May God attend our plans!"

One by one they withdrew, until only Catesby was left.

"You've not moved, Guy. Is anything wrong?"

"I must have time to think on this," said Faulkner.

"Ten days, no more. The calendar marks the twenty-fifth of the month. In six more, November's upon us, and within the week beyond that James and Salisbury will be no more!" He stuck out his hand to shake Faulkner's. "Good luck, Guy. We'll to victory or hang with you." At the threshold he turned for a final word. "I trust when again we meet at this place, 'twill be Old Paradise no longer, but New!"

Then he was gone.

Faulkner sat alone and, for the moment, unmoving. How quixotic were his thoughts! Were it possible for a man to step back into time, he might have done so. The time would be 1605, the event the Gunpowder Plot against James I and Lord Salisbury. But in his mind was a core of turgid confusion. How was it possible for him to remember so well these people with whom he had sat this night and yet never met?

Was there, indeed, a hoax that intended him for victim? Or was there, on the other hand, a danger that there was indeed some plan afoot to blow up Parliament? He grew cold with fear. Something must be done to prevent such a plan's fulfilment. But what?

Who was it had mentioned Tresham and Lord Monteagle?

He looked wildly about him; there was not much time. At any moment he might be interrupted. The householder might come back. Wright, it seemed, was owner here. Or was it but another of Catesby's houses?

He came upon paper, a quill pen, ink.

"My lord, out of the love I bear to some of your friends, I have a care for preservation. Therefore I would advise you, as you tender your life, to devise some excuse to shift of your attendance of this Parliament, for God and man hath concurred to punish the wickedness of this time. And think not slightly of this advertisement, but retire yourself into your country, where you may expect the event in safety, for though there be no appearance of any stir, yet I say they shall receive a terrible blow, the Parliament, and yet they shall not see who hurts them. This counsel is not to be condemned, because it may do you good and can do you no harm, for the danger is past as soon as you have burnt the letter, and I hope God will give you the grace to make good use of it, to whose holy protection I commend you."

Without hesitation, he signed it, "Tresham". His own name would have no meaning to Lord Monteagle. He folded the letter, folded another paper around it so devised to hold it as might an envelope, of which he saw none, wrote Lord Monteagle's name in a bold hand on the outside, and, without another glance for his surroundings, fled the room, fled the next, and in a few moments was outside and running through the fog as fast as possible, until he found a postman's box, and there dropped his letter, trusting that it would reach Monteagle in time. Ten days. He felt for his lighter, but he had left it, as he had his hat. He would not retrace his steps.

The air stirred him, the close-pressing fog brought him once again to awareness that he was lost. But no, not quite; was that not Westminster Bridge ahead? He walked on, and soon found himself above the Thames, with the fog beginning to thin.

Though it was past midnight, Gunter was still waiting for him. Not because he had intended to do so, but because he had fallen asleep in Faulkner's room. He started awake under Faulkner's touch.

"I've been asleep," he said, ruefully, looking at his watch. "And missed a nightcap with Barry."

"Have one with me," said Faulkner, moving towards the decanter. "I've had an evening."

"In this fog!"

"It's beginning to lift." Faulkner came back with glasses and the decanter. "What have you found?"

"Ah, something of interest, indeed," said Gunter, becoming alert at once. "Though I've no way of knowing how you'll take it." He tossed off a drink and complimented Faulkner. "It's all in these papers." He took them out of his pocket, tapped them intimately where he held them in his hand, and gave them to Faulkner.

"I've got you back as far as York. The name was changed, you see, in 1605. Used to be Fawkes. Family of Edward Fawkes of York. It was Edward's son Guy . . ."

"The Gunpowder Plot!"

"Of course. The disgrace of it upon the family brought about the change in name. One understands that, of course. But no doubt you Americans look upon these things in a more romantic light."

Faulkner's mouth went dry; his whisky was tasteless on his tongue.

He opened the papers and read of the succession of the line of Edward Fawkes, father of Guy Fawkes, who lent his name forever to the Gunpowder Plot to blow up Parliament with King James I and his ministers . . .

In the clear light of morning, he knew what he must do. He had a perfect excuse – to look for his hat and lighter. True, he did not know the address, but had not one of them spoken of "Old Paradise", and was there not a street by that name not far from the Thames, off Westminster Bridge?

On that chance he called a cab. "Take me to Old Paradise Street."

There was no question. He got in, settled back, and was soon rolling towards his destination. The number, he remembered, was 16.

Someone had made game of him for Hallowe'en – which

was odd, for not many of the British celebrated All Hallows. Who they were, Faulkner would soon know. There was no fog this morning to confuse him.

The cab rolled over Westminster Bridge and soon after came to a halt.

"Old Paradise, sir," said the driver.

Faulkner got out, paid him and let him go. He walked slowly up the street. He could hardly hope to find any familiar facet, for the thick fog of the preceding evening had shrouded everything unrecognizably. Even the walk beneath his feet felt different. It had had the feel of cobbles in the night.

A short street. But there was no number 16.

He stood for a moment puzzled. But a postman coming along gave him hope and he stopped him.

"Number 16?" said the postman. "I'm old enough to remember that. Before the war. It's rubble now. Come along, I'll show you where it was."

Faulkner followed him, and they came presently to a cellar filled with rubble. There had once been a house there, and steps leading up to it, and iron railings about it. The railings were still there. Beyond, all was rubble. But not far from where they stood, in the rubble, lay the same numerals Faulkner had seen less than a day ago – not bright and gleaming now, but old, worn, bent. And beyond that . . . ?

"They've not got around to clean up here yet," said the postman apologetically. "The place was hit not long after Coventry. Historic house, too. Said to have been used as a meeting place for the Gunpowder Plotters. Oh, I say now, you'd better not go climbing about in that rubble, sir – it's posted as dangerous."

But Faulkner had gone ahead.

He felt he had the best right in the world to do so. Hoax, hallucination, dream – whatever had happened to him, he meant to retrieve his hat and the lighter which lay gleaming not far from it in the middle of the ruin and a little towards the rear – just where the room with the table would have been – if there had been such a room – and such a house. . . . New Paradise indeed!

He went back to his hotel and telephoned Inigo Gunter.

"Tell me, did they ever find out who wrote that letter to Lord Monteagle in the Gunpowder affair?"

"No, Mr Faulkner, to the best of my knowledge, they did not. They thought it was Tresham, but he denied it and died in the Tower. He might have won his freedom."

"Never mind, Mr Gunter, I did it myself."

That was a break he had not meant to make, he told himself after he had been cut off. He had meant to voice his belief that Guy Fawkes had written to Monteagle and disclosed the plot. But to call Gunter again and explain would only complicate matters more.

Inigo Gunter entertained his colleagues for weeks with his anecdote about the mad American and his delusion.

Phantas

OLIVER ONIONS

I

As Abel Keeling lay on the galleon's deck, held from rolling down it only by his own weight and the sun-blackened hand that lay outstretched upon the planks, his gaze wandered, but ever returned to the bell that hung jammed with the dangerous heel-over of the vessel, in the small ornamental belfry immediately abaft the mainmast. The bell was of cast bronze, with half-obliterated bosses upon it that had been the heads of cherubs; but wind and salt spray had given it a thick incrustation of bright, beautiful, lichenous green. It was this colour that Abel Keeling's eyes liked.

For wherever else on the galleon his eyes rested they found only whiteness – the whiteness of extreme eld. There were slightly varying degrees in her whiteness; here she was of a white that glistened like salt-granules, there of a greyish chalky white, and again her whiteness had the yellowish cast of decay; but everywhere it was the mild, disquieting whiteness of materials out of which the life had departed. Her cordage was bleached as old straw is bleached, and half her ropes kept their shape little more firmly than the ash of a string keeps it shape after the fire has passed; her pallid timbers were white and clean as bones found in sand; and even the wild frankincense with which (for lack of tar, at her last touching of land) she had been pitched, had dried to a pale hard gum that sparkled like quartz in her open seams. The sun was yet so pale a buckler of silver through the still white mists that not a cord or timber cast a shadow; and only Abel Keeling's face and hands were black, carked and cinder-black from exposure to his pitiless rays.

The galleon was the *Mary of the Tower*, and she had a frightful list to starboard. So canted was she that her mainyard dipped one of its steel sickles into the glassy water, and, had her foremast remained, or more than the broken stump of her bonaventure mizzen, she must have turned over completely. Many days ago they had stripped the mainyard of its course, and had passed the sail under the *Mary*'s bottom, in the hope that it would stop the leak. This it had partly done as long as the galleon had continued to glide one way; then, without coming about, she had begun to glide the other, the ropes had parted, and she had dragged the sail after her, leaving a broad tarnish on the silver sea.

For it was broadside that the galleon glided, almost imperceptibly, ever sucking down. She glided as if a loadstone drew her, and, at first, Abel Keeling had thought it was a loadstone, pulling at her iron, drawing her through the pearly mists that lay like face-cloths to the water and hid at a short distance the tarnish left by the sail. But later he had known that it was no loadstone drawing at her iron. The motion was due – must be due – to the absolute deadness of the calm in that silent, sinister, three-miles-broad waterway. With the eye of his mind he saw that loadstone now as he lay against a gun-truck, all but toppling down the deck. Soon that would happen again which had happened for five days past. He would hear again the chattering of monkeys and the screaming of parrots, the mat of green and yellow weeds would creep in towards the *Mary* over the quicksilver sea, once more the sheer wall of rock would rise, and the men would run . . .

But no; the men would not run this time to drop the fenders. There were no men left to do so, unless Bligh was still alive. Perhaps Bligh was still alive. He had walked half-way down the quarter-deck steps a little before the sudden nightfall of the day before, had then fallen and lain for a minute (dead, Abel Keeling had supposed, watching him from his place by the gun-truck), and had then got up again and tottered forward to the forecastle, his tall figure swaying, and his long arms waving. Abel Keeling had not seen him since. Most likely, he had died in the forecastle during the night. If he had not been dead he would have come aft again for water . . .

At the remembrance of the water Abel Keeling lifted his head. The strands of lean muscle about his emaciated mouth worked, and he made a little pressure of his sun-blackened hand on the deck, as if to verify its steepness and his own balance. The mainmast was some seven or eight yards away . . . He put one stiff leg under him and began, seated as he was, to make shuffling movements down the slope.

To the mainmast, near the belfry, was affixed his contrivance for catching water. It consisted of a collar of rope set lower at one side than at the other (but that had been before the mast had steeved so many degrees away from the zenith), and tallowed beneath. The mists lingered later in that gully of a strait than they did on the open ocean, and the collar of rope served as a collector for the dews that condensed on the masts. The drops fell into a small earthen pipkin placed on the deck beneath it.

Abel Keeling reached the pipkin and looked into it. It was nearly a third full of fresh water. Good. If Bligh, the mate, was dead, so much the more water for Abel Keeling, master of the *Mary of the Tower*. He dipped two fingers into the pipkin and put them into his mouth. This he did several times. He did not dare to raise the pipkin to his black and broken lips for dread of a remembered agony, he could not have told how many days ago, when a devil had whispered to him, and he had gulped down the contents of the pipkin in the morning, and for the rest of the day had gone waterless . . . Again he moistened his fingers and sucked them; then he lay sprawling against the mast, idly watching the drops of water as they fell.

It was odd how the drops formed. Slowly they collected at the edge of the tallowed collar, trembled in their fullness for an instant, and fell, another beginning the process instantly. It amused Abel Keeling to watch them. Why (he wondered) were all the drops the same size? What cause and compulsion did they obey that they never varied, and what frail tenuity held the little globules intact? It must be due to some Cause . . . He remembered that the aromatic gum of the wild frankincense with which they had parcelled the seams had hung on the buckets in great sluggish gouts, obedient to a different compulsion; oil was different again, and so were juices and balsams. Only quicksilver (perhaps the heavy and motionless sea put him in mind of quicksilver) seemed obedient to no law . . . Why was it so?

Bligh, of course, would have had his explanation: it was the Hand of God. That sufficed for Bligh, who had gone forward the evening before, and whom Abel Keeling now seemed vaguely and as at a distance to remember as the deep-voiced fanatic who had sung his hymns as, man by man, he committed the bodies of the ship's company to the deep. Bligh was that sort of man; accepted things without question; was content to take things as they were and be ready with the fenders when the wall of rock rose out of the opalescent mists. Bligh, too, like the waterdrops, had his Law, that was his and nobody else's . . .

There floated down from some rotten rope up aloft a flake of scurf, that settled in the pipkin. Abel Keeling watched it dully as it settled towards the pipkin's rim. When presently he again dipped his fingers into the vessel the water ran into a little vortex, drawing the flake with it. The water settled again; and again the minute flake determined towards the rim and adhered there, as if the rim had power to draw it . . .

It was exactly so that the galleon was gliding towards the wall of rock, the yellow and green weeds, and the monkeys and parrots. Put out into mid-water again (while there had been men to put her out) she had glided to the other wall. One force drew the chip in the pipkin and the ship over the tranced sea. It was the Hand of God, said Bligh . . .

Abel Keeling, his mind now noting minute things and now clouded with torpor, did not at first hear a voice that was quakingly lifted up over by the forecastle – a voice that drew nearer, to an accompaniment of swirling water.

"O Thou, that Jonas in the fish
Three days didst keep from pain,
Which was a figure of Thy death
And rising up again—"

It was Bligh, singing one of his hymns:

"O Thou, that Noah keptst from flood
And Abram, day by day,
As he along through Egypt passed
Didst guide him in the way—"

The voice ceased, leaving the pious period uncompleted. Bligh was alive, at any rate . . . Abel Keeling resumed his fitful musing.

Yes, that was the Law of Bligh's life, to call things the Hand of God; but Abel Keeling's Law was different; no better, no worse, only different. The Hand of God, that drew ships and galleons, must work by some method; and Abel Keeling's eyes were dully on the pipkin again as if he sought the method there . . .

Then conscious thought left him for a space, and when he resumed it was without obvious connection.

Oars, of course, were the thing. With oars, men could laugh at calms. Oars, that only pinnaces and galliasses now used, had had their advantages. But oars (which was to say a method, for you could say if you liked that the Hand of God grasped the oar-loom, as the Breath of God filled the sail) – oars were antiquated, belonged to the past, meant a throwing-over of all that was good and new and a return to fine lines, a battle-formation abreast to give effect to the shock of the ram, and a day or two at sea and then to port again for provisions. Oars . . . no. Abel Keeling was one of the new men, the men who swore by the line-ahead, the broadside fire of sakers and demi-cannon, and weeks and months without a landfall. Perhaps one day the wits of such men as he would devise a craft, not oar-driven (because oars could not penetrate into the remote seas of the world) – not sail-driven (because men who trusted to sails found themselves in an airless, three-mile strait, suspended motionless between cloud and water, ever gliding to a wall of rock) – but a ship . . . a ship . . .

"To Noah and his sons with him
God spake, and thus said He:
A cov'nant set I up with you
And your posterity—"

It was Bligh again, wandering somewhere in the waist. Abel Keeling's mind was once more a blank. Then slowly, slowly, as the water drops collected on the collar of rope, his thought took shape again.

A galliasse? No, not a galliasse. The galliasse made shift to be two things, and was neither. This ship, that the hand of man should one day make for the Hand of God to manage, should be a ship that should take and conserve the force of the wind, take it and store it as she stored her victuals; at rest when she wished, going ahead when she wished; turning the forces both of calm and storm against themselves. For, of course, her force must be wind – stored wind – a bag of the winds, as the children's tale had it – wind probably directed upon the water astern, driving it away and urging forward the ship, acting by reaction. She would have a wind-chamber, into which wind would be pumped with pumps. Bligh would call that equally the Hand of God, this driving-force of the ship of the future that Abel Keeling dimly foreshadowed as he lay between the mainmast and the belfry, turning his eyes now and then from ashy white timbers to the vivid green bronze-rust of the bell above him . . .

Bligh's face, liver-coloured with the sun and ravaged from inwards by the faith that consumed him, appeared at the head of the quarter-deck steps. His voice beat uncontrolledly out.

"And in the earth here is no place
Of refuge to be found,
Nor in the deep and water-course
That passeth under ground—"

II

Bligh's eyes were lidded, as if in contemplation of his inner ecstasy. His head was thrown back, and his brows worked up and down tormentedly. His wide mouth remained open as his hymn was suddenly interrupted on the long-drawn note. From somewhere in the shimmering mists the note was taken up, and there drummed and rang and reverberated through the strait a windy, hoarse, and dismal bellow, alarming and sustained. A tremor rang through Bligh. Moving like a sightless man, he stumbled forward from the head of the quarter-deck steps, and Abel Keeling was aware of his gaunt figure behind him, taller for the steepness of the deck. As that vast empty sound died away, Bligh laughed in his mania.

"Lord, hath the grave's wide mouth a tongue to praise Thee? Lo, again—"

Again the cavernous sound possessed the air, louder and nearer. Through it came another sound, a slow throb, throb – throb, throb – Again the sounds ceased.

"Even Leviathan lifted up his voice in praise!" Bligh sobbed.

Abel Keeling did not raise his head. There had returned to him the memory of that day when, before the morning mists had lifted from the strait, he had emptied the pipkin of the water that was the allowance until night should fall again. During that agony of thirst he had seen shapes and heard sounds with other than his mortal eyes and ears, and even in the moments that had alternated with his lightness, when he had known these to be hallucinations, they had come again. He had heard the bells on a Sunday in his own Kentish home, the calling of children at play, the unconcerned singing of men at their daily labour, and the laughter and gossip of the women as they had spread the linen on the hedge or distributed bread upon the platters. These voices had rung in his brain, interrupted now and then by the groans of Bligh and of two other men who had been alive then. Some of the voices he had heard had been silent on earth this many a long year, but Abel Keeling, thirst-tortured, had heard them, even as he was now hearing that vacant moaning with the intermittent throbbing that filled the strait with alarm . . .

"Praise Him, praise Him, praise Him!" Bligh was calling deliriously.

Then a bell seemed to sound in Abel Keeling's ears, and, as if something in the mechanism of his brain had slipped, another picture rose in his fancy – the scene when the *Mary of the Tower* had put out, to a bravery of swinging bells and shrill fifes and valiant trumpets. She had not been a leper-white galleon then. The scroll-work on her prow had twinkled with gilding; her belfry and stern-galleries and elaborate lanterns had flashed in the sun with gold; and her fighting-tops and the warpavesse about her waist had been gay with painted coats and scutcheons. To her sails had been stitched gaudy ramping lions of scarlet say, and from her mainyard, now dipping in the water, had hung the broad two-tailed pennant with the Virgin and Child embroidered upon it . . .

Then suddenly a voice about him seemed to be saying, "*And a half-seven – and a half-seven—*" and in a twink the picture in Abel Keeling's brain changed again. He was at home again, instructing his son, young Abel, in the casting of the lead from the skiff they had pulled out of the harbour.

"*And a half-seven!*" the boy seemed to be calling.

Abel Keeling's blackened lips muttered: "Excellently well cast, Abel, excellently well cast!"

"*And a half-seven – and a half-seven – seven – seven—*"

"Ah," Abel Keeling murmured, "that last was not a clear cast – give me the line – thus it should go . . . ay, so . . . Soon you shall sail the seas with me in the *Mary of the Tower*. You are already perfect in the stars and the motions of the planets; tomorrow I will instruct you in the use of the backstaff . . ."

For a minute or two he continued to mutter; then he dozed. When again he came to semi-consciousness it was once more to the sounds of bells, at first faint, then louder, and finally becoming a noisy clamour immediately above his head. It was Bligh. Bligh, in a fresh attack of delirium, had seized the bell-lanyard and was ringing the bell insanely. The cord broke in his fingers, but he thrust at the bell with his hand, and again called aloud.

"Upon a harp and an instrument of ten strings . . . let Heaven and Earth praise Thy Name! . . ."

He continued to call aloud, and to beat on the bronze-rusted bell.

"Ship ahoy! What ship's that?"

One would have said that a veritable hail had come out of the mists, but Abel Keeling knew those hails that came out of the mists. They came from ships which were not there. "Ay, ay, keep a good look-out, and have a care to your lode-manage," he muttered again to his son . . .

But, as sometimes a sleeper sits up in his dream, or rises from his couch and walks, so all of a sudden Abel Keeling found himself on his hands and knees on the deck, looking back over his shoulder. In some deep-seated region of his consciousness he was dimly aware that the cant of the deck had become more perilous, but his brain received the intelligence and forgot it again. He was looking out into the bright and baffling mists. The buckler of the sun was of a more ardent silver; the sea below it was lost in brilliant evaporation; and between them, suspended in the haze, no more substantial than the vague darknesses that float before dazzled eyes, a pyramidal phantom-shape hung. Abel Keeling passed his hand over his eyes, but when he removed it the shape was still there, gliding slowly towards the *Mary*'s quarter. Its form changed as he watched it. The spirit-grey shape that had been a pyramid seemed to dissolve into four upright members, slightly graduated in tallness, that nearest the *Mary*'s stern the tallest and that to the left the lowest. It might have been the shadow of the gigantic set of reed-pipes on which that vacant mournful note had been sounded.

And as he looked, with fooled eyes, again his ears became fooled:

"Ahoy there! What ship's that? Are you a ship? . . . Here, give me that trumpet—" Then a metallic barking. *"Ahoy there! What the devil are you? Didn't you ring a bell?*

Ring it again, or blow a blast or something, and go dead slow!"

All this came, as it were, indistinctly, and though a sort of high singing in Abel Keeling's own ears. Then he fancied a short bewildered laugh, followed by a colloquy from somewhere between sea and sky.

"Here, Ward, just pinch me, will you? Tell me what you see there. I want to know if I'm awake."

"See where?"

"There, on the starboard bow. (Stop that ventilating fan; I can't hear myself think.) See anything? Don't tell me it's that damned Dutchman – don't pitch me that old Vanderdecken tale – give me an easy one first, something about a sea-serpent . . . You did hear that bell, didn't you?"

"Shut up a minute – listen—"

Again Bligh's voice was lifted up.

> "This is the cov'nant that I make:
> From henceforth nevermore
> Will I again the world destroy
> With water, as before."

Bligh's voice died away again in Abel Keeling's ears.

"Oh – my – fat – Aunt – Julia!" the voice that seemed to come from between sea and sky sounded again. Then it spoke more loudly. "*I say,*" it began with careful politeness, "*if you are a ship, do you mind telling us where the masquerade is to be? Our wireless is out of order, and we hadn't heard of it . . . Oh, you do see it, Ward, don't you? . . . Please, please tell us what the hell you are!*"

Again Abel Keeling had moved as a sleep-walker moves. He had raised himself up by the belfry timbers, and Bligh had sunk in a heap on the deck. Abel Keeling's movement overturned the pipkin, which raced the little trickle of its contents down the deck and lodged where the still and brimming sea made, as it were, a chain with the carved balustrade of the quarter-deck – one link a still gleaming edge, then a dark baluster, and then another gleaming link. For one moment only Abel Keeling found himself noticing that that which had driven Bligh aft had been the rising of the water in the waist as the galleon settled by the head – the waist was now entirely submerged; then once more he was absorbed in his dream, its voices, and its shape in the mist, which had again taken the form of a pyramid before his eyeballs.

"*Of course*," a voice seemed to be complaining anew, and still through that confused dinning in Abel Keeling's ears, "*we can't turn a four-inch on it . . . And, of course, Ward, I don't believe in 'em. D'you hear, Ward? I don't believe in 'em, I say . . . Shall we call down to old A.B.? This might interest His Scientific Skippership . . .*"

"*Oh, lower a boat and pull out to it – into it – over it – through it—*"

"*Look at our chaps crowded on the barbette yonder. They've seen it. Better not give an order you know won't be obeyed . . .*"

Abel Keeling, cramped against the antique belfry, had begun to find his dream interesting. For, though he did not know her build, that mirage was the shape of a ship. No doubt it was projected from his brooding on ships of half an hour before; and that was odd . . . But perhaps, after all, it was not very odd. He knew that she did not really exist; only the appearance of her existed; but things had to exist like that before they really existed. Before the *Mary of the Tower* had existed she had been a shape in some man's imagination; before that, some dreamer had dreamed the form of a ship with oars; and before that, far away in the dawn and infancy of the world, some seer had seen in a vision the raft before man had ventured to push out over the water on his two planks. And since this shape that rode before Abel Keeling's eyes was a shape in his, Abel Keeling's dream, he, Abel Keeling, was the master of it. His own brooding brain had contrived her, and she was launched upon the illimitable ocean of his own mind . . .

"And I will not unmindful be
Of this, My cov'nant, passed

Twixt Me and you and every flesh
Whiles that the world should last,"

sang Bligh, rapt . . .

But as a dreamer, even in his dream, will scratch upon the wall by his couch some key or word to put him in mind of his vision on the morrow when it has left him, so Abel Keeling found himself seeking some sign to be a proof to those to whom no vision is vouchsafed. Even Bligh sought that – could not be silent in his bliss, but lay on the deck there, uttering great passionate Amens and praising his Maker, as he said, upon a harp and an instrument of ten strings. So with Abel Keeling. It would be the Amen of his life to have praised God, not upon a harp, but upon a ship that should carry her own power, that should store wind or its equivalent as she stored her victuals, that should be something wrested from the chaos of uninvention and ordered and disciplined and subordinated to Abel Keeling's will . . . And there she was, that ship-shaped thing of spirit-grey, with the four pipes that resembled a phantom organ now broadside and of equal length. And the ghost-crew of that ship were speaking again . . .

The interrupted silver chain by the quarter-deck balustrade had now become continuous, and the balusters made a herring-bone over their own motionless reflections. The spilt water from the pipkin had dried, and the pipkin was not to be seen. Abel Keeling stood beside the mast, erect as God made man to go. With his leathery hand he smote upon the bell. He waited for the space of a minute, and then cried:

"Ahoy! . . . Ship ahoy! . . . What ship's that?

III

We are not conscious in a dream that we are playing a game, the beginning and end of which are in ourselves. In this dream of Abel Keeling's a voice replied:

"*Hallo, it's found its tongue . . . Ahoy there! What are you?*"

Loudly and in a clear voice Abel Keeling called: "Are you a ship?"

With a nervous giggle the answer came:

"*We are a ship, aren't we, Ward? I hardly feel sure . . . Yes, of course, we're a ship. No question about us. The question is what the dickens you are.*"

Not all the words these voices used were intelligible to Abel Keeling, and he knew not what it was in the tone of these last words that reminded him of the honour due to the *Mary of the Tower*. Blister-white and at the end of her life as she was, Abel Keeling was still jealous of her dignity; the voice had a youngish ring; and it was not fitting that young chins should be wagged about his galleon. He spoke curtly.

"You that spoke – are you the master of that ship?"

"*Officer of the watch,*" the words floated back; "*the captain's below.*"

"Then send for him. It is with masters that masters hold speech," Abel Keeling replied.

He could see the two shapes, flat and without relief, standing on a high narrow structure with rails. One of them gave a low whistle, and seemed to be fanning his face; but the other rumbled something into a sort of funnel. Presently the two shapes became three. There was a murmuring, as of a consultation, and then suddenly a new voice spoke. At its thrill and tone a sudden tremor ran through Abel Keeling's frame. He wondered what response it was that that voice found in the forgotten recesses of his memory.

"*Ahoy!*" seemed to call this new yet faintly remembered voice.

"*What's all this about? Listen. We're His Majesty's destroyer* Seapink, *out of Devonport last October, and nothing particular the matter with us. Now who are you?*"

"The *Mary of the Tower*, out of the Port of Rye on the day of Saint Anne, and only two men—"

A gasp interrupted him.

"*Out of* WHERE?" that voice that so strangely moved Abel

Keeling said unsteadily, while Bligh broke into groans of renewed rapture.

"Out of the Port of Rye, in the County of Sussex . . . nay, give ear, else I cannot make you hear me while this man's spirit and flesh wrestle so together! . . . Ahoy! Are you gone?" For the voices had become a low murmur, and the ship-shape had faded before Abel Keeling's eyes. Again and again he called. He wished to be informed of the disposition and economy of the wind-chamber . . .

"The wind-chamber!" he called, in an agony lest the knowledge almost within his grasp should be lost. "I would know about the wind-chamber . . ."

Like an echo, there came back the words, uncomprehendingly uttered, "*The wind-chamber? . . .*"

". . . that driveth the vessel – perchance 'tis not wind – a steel bow that is bent also conserveth force – the force you store, to move at will through calm and storm . . ."

"*Can you make out what it's driving at?*"

"*Oh, we shall all wake up in a minute . . .*"

"*Quiet, I have it; the engines; it wants to know about our engines. It'll be wanting to see our papers presently. Rye Port! . . . Well, no harm in humouring it; let's see what it can make of this. Ahoy there!*" came the voice to Abel Keeling, a little strongly, as if a shifting wind carried, and speaking faster and faster as it went on. "*Not wind, but steam; d'you hear? Steam, steam. Steam, in eight Yarrow water-tube boilers. S-t-e-a-m, steam. Got it? And we've twin-screw triple expansion engines, indicated horse-power four thousand, and we can do 430 revolutions per minute; savvy? Is there anything your phantomhood would like to know about our armament? . . .*"

Abel Keeling was muttering fretfully to himself. It annoyed him that words in his own vision should have no meaning for him. How did words come to him in a dream that he had no knowledge of when wide awake? The *Seapink* – that was the name of this ship; but a pink was long and narrow, low-carged and square-built aft . . .

"*And as for our armament,*" the voice with the tones that so profoundly troubled Abel Keeling's memory continued, "*we've two revolving Whitehead torpedo-tubes, three six-pounders on the upper deck, and that's a twelve-pounder forward there by the conning-tower. I forgot to mention that we're nickel steel, with a coal capacity of sixty tons in most damnably placed bunkers, and that thirty and a quarter knots is about our top. Care to come aboard?*"

But the voice was speaking still more rapidly and feverishly, as if to fill a silence with no matter what, and the shape that was uttering it was straining forward anxiously over the rail.

"*Ugh! But I'm glad this happened in the daylight,*" another voice was muttering.

"*I wish I was sure it was happening at all . . . Poor old spook!*"

"*I suppose it would keep its feet if her deck was quite vertical. Think she'll go down, or just melt?*"

"*Kind of go down . . . without wash . . .*"

"*Listen – here's the other one now—*"

For Bligh was singing again:

"For, Lord, Thou know'st our nature such
  If we great things obtain,
And in the getting of the same
  Do feel no grief or pain,

"We little do esteem thereof;
  But, hardly brought to pass,
A thousand times we do esteem
  More than the other was."

"*But oh, look – look – look at the other! . . . Oh, I say, wasn't he a grand old boy! Look!*"

For, transfiguring Abel Keeling's form as a prophet's form is transfigured in the instant of his rapture, flooding his brain with the white eureka-light of perfect knowledge, that for which he and his dream had been at a standstill had come. He knew her, this ship of the future, as if God's Finger had bitten her lines into his brain. He knew her as those already sinking into the grave know things, miraculously, completely, accepting Life's impossibilities with a nodded "Of course". From the ardent mouths of her eight furnaces to the last drip from her lubricators, from her bed-plates to the breeches of her quick-firers, he knew her – read her gauges, thumbed her bearings, gave the ranges from her range-finders, and lived the life he lived who was in command of her. And he would not forget on the morrow, as he had forgotten on many morrows, for at last he had seen the water about his feet, and knew that there would be no morrow for him in this world . . .

And even in that moment, with but a sand or two to run in his glass, indomitable, insatiable, dreaming dream on dream, he could not die until he knew more. He had two questions to ask, and a master-question; and but a moment remained. Sharply his voice rang out.

"Ho, there! . . . This ancient ship, the *Mary of the Tower*, cannot steam thirty and a quarter knots, but yet she can sail the waters. What more does your ship? Can she soar above them, as the fowls of the air soar?"

"*Lord, he thinks we're an aeroplane! . . . No, she can't . . .*"

"And can you dive, even as the fishes of the deep?"

"*No . . . Those are submarines . . . we aren't a submarine . . .*"

But Abel Keeling waited for no more. He gave an exulting chuckle.

"Oho, oho – thirty knots, and but on the face of the waters – no more than that? Oho! . . . Now *my* ship, the ship I see as a mother sees full-grown the child she has but conceived – *my* ship I say – oho! – *my* ship shall . . . Below there – trip that gun!"

The cry came suddenly and alertly, as a muffled sound came from below and an ominous tremor shook the galleon.

"*By Jove, her guns are breaking loose below – that's her finish—*"

"Trip that gun, and double-breech the others!" Abel Keeling's voice rang out, as if there had been any to obey him. He had braced himself within the belfry frame; and then in the middle of the next order his voice suddenly failed him. His ship-shape, that for the moment he had forgotten, rode once more before his eyes. This was the end, and his master-question, apprehension for the answer to which was now torturing his face and well-nigh bursting his heart, was still unasked.

"Ho – he that spoke with me – the master," he cried in a voice that ran high, "is he there?"

"*Yes, yes!*" came the other voice across the water, sick with suspense. "*Oh, be quick!*"

There was a moment in which hoarse cries from many voices, a heavy thud and rumble on wood, and a crash of timbers and a gurgle and a splash were indescribably mingled; the gun under which Abel Keeling had lain had snapped her rotten breechings and plunged down the deck, carrying Bligh's unconscious form with it. The deck came up vertical, and for one instant longer Abel Keeling clung to the belfry.

"I cannot see your face," he screamed, "but meseems your voice is a voice I know. *What is your name?*"

In a torn sob the answer came across the water:

"*Keeling – Abel Keeling . . . Oh, my God!*"

And Abel Keeling's cry of triumph, that mounted to a victorious "Huzza!" was lost in the downward plunge of the *Mary of the Tower*, that left the strait empty save for the sun's fiery blaze and the last smoke-like evaporation of the mists.

The New Accelerator

H. G. WELLS

Certainly, if ever a man found a guinea when he was looking for a pin it is my good friend Professor Gibberne. I have heard before of investigators overshooting the mark, but never quite to the extent that he has done. He has really, this time at any rate, without any touch of exaggeration in the phrase, found something to revolutionise human life. And that when he was simply seeking an all-round nervous stimulant to bring languid people up to the stresses of these pushful days. I have tasted the stuff now several times, and I cannot do better than describe the effect the thing had on me. That there are astonishing experiences in store for all in search of new sensations will become apparent enough.

Professor Gibberne, as many people know, is my neighbour in Folkestone. Unless my memory plays me a trick, his portrait at various ages has already appeared in *The Strand Magazine* – I think late in 1899; but I am unable to look it up because I have lent that volume to someone who has never sent it back. The reader may, perhaps, recall the high forehead and the singularly long black eyebrows that give such a Mephistophelian touch to his face. He occupies one of those pleasant detached houses in the mixed style that make the western end of Upper Sandgate Road so interesting. His is the one with the Flemish gables and the Moorish portico, and it is in the room with the mullioned bay window that he works when he is down here, and in which of an evening we have so often smoked and talked together. He is a mighty jester, but besides, he likes to talk to me about his work; he is one of those men who find a help and stimulus in talking, and so I have been able to follow the conception of the New Accelerator right up from a very early stage. Of course, the greater portion of his experimental work is not done in Folkestone, but in Gower Street, in the new laboratory next to the hospital that he has been the first to use.

As everyone knows, or at least as all intelligent people know, the special department in which Gibberne has gained so great and deserved a reputation among physiologists is the action of drugs upon the nervous system. Upon soporifics, sedatives, and anaesthetics he is, I am told, unequalled. He is also a chemist of considerable eminence, and I suppose in the subtle and complex jungle of riddles that centres about the ganglion cell and the axis fibre there are little cleared places of his making, glades of illumination, that, until he sees fit to publish his results, are inaccessible to every other living man. And the last few years he has been particularly assiduous upon this question of nervous stimulants, and already, before the discovery of the New Accelerator, very successful with them. Medical science has to thank him for at least three distinct and absolutely safe invigorators of unrivalled value to practising men. In cases of exhaustion the preparation known as Gibberne's B Syrup has I suppose, saved more lives already than any lifeboat round the coast.

"But none of these things begin to satisfy me yet," he told me nearly a year ago. "Either they increase the central energy without affecting the nerves or they simply increase the available energy by lowering the nervous conductivity; and all of them are unequal and local in their operation. One wakes up the heart and viscera and leaves the brain stupefied, one gets at the brain champagne fashion and does nothing good for the solar plexus, and what I want – and what, if it's an early possibility, I mean to have – is a stimulant that stimulates all round, that wakes you up for a time from the crown of your head to the tip of your great toe, and makes you go two – or even three – to everybody else's one. Eh? That's the thing I'm after."

"It would tire a man," I said.

"Not a doubt of it. And you'd eat double or treble – and all that. But just think what the thing would mean. Imagine yourself with a little phial like this" – he held up a bottle of green glass and marked his points with it – "and in the precious phial is the power to think twice as fast, move twice as quickly, do twice as much work in a given time as you could otherwise do."

"But is such a thing possible?"

"I believe so. If it isn't, I've wasted my time for a year. These various preparations of the hypophosphites, for example, seem to show that something of the sort . . . Even if it was only one and half times as fast it would do."

"It *would* do," I said.

"If you were a statesman in a corner, for example, time rushing up against you, something urgent to be done, eh?"

"He could dose his private secretary," I said.

"And gain – double time. And think if you, for example, wanted to finish a book."

"Usually," I said, "I wish I'd never begun 'em."

"Or a doctor, driven to death, wants to sit down and think out a case. Or a barrister – or a man cramming for an examination."

"Worth a guinea a drop," said I, "and more – to men like that."

"And in a duel again," said Gibberne, "where it all depends on your quickness in pulling the trigger."

"Or in fencing," I echoed.

"You see," said Gibberne, "if I get it as an all-round thing it will really do you no harm at all – except perhaps to an infinitesimal degree it brings you nearer old age. You will just have lived twice to other people's once—"

"I suppose," I meditated, "in a duel – it would be fair?"

"That's a question for the seconds," said Gibberne.

I harked back further. "And you really think such a thing *is* possible?" I said.

"As possible," said Gibberne, and glanced at something that went throbbing by the window, "as a motor-bus. As a matter of fact—"

He paused and smiled at me deeply, and tapped slowly on the edge of his desk with the green phial. "I think I know the stuff. . . . Already I've got something coming." The nervous smile upon his face betrayed the gravity of his revelation. He rarely talked of his actual experimental work unless things were very near the end. "And it may be, it may – I shouldn't be surprised – it may even do the thing at a greater rate than twice."

"It will be rather a big thing," I hazarded.

"It will be, I think, rather a big thing."

But I don't think he quite knew what a big thing it was to be, for all that.

I remember we had several subsequent talks about the stuff. "The New Accelerator" he called it, and his tone about it grew more confident on each occasion. Sometimes he talked nervously of unexpected physiological results its use might have, and then he would get a bit unhappy; at others he was frankly mercenary, and we debated long and anxiously how the preparation might be turned to commercial account. "It's a good thing," said Gibberne, "a tremendous thing. I know I'm giving the world something, and I think it only reasonable we should expect the world to pay. The dignity of science is all very well, but I think somehow I must have the monopoly of the stuff for, say, ten years. I don't see why *all* the fun in life should go to the dealers in ham."

My own interest in the coming drug certainly did not wane in the time. I have always had a queer twist towards metaphysics in my mind. I have always been given to paradoxes about space and time, and it seemed to me that Gibberne was really preparing no less than the absolute acceleration of life. Suppose a man repeatedly dosed with such a preparation: he would live an active and record life indeed, but he would be an adult at eleven, middle-aged at twenty-five, and by thirty well on the road to senile decay. It seemed to me that so far Gibberne was only going to do for anyone who took this drug exactly what Nature has done for the Jews and Orientals, who are men in their teens and aged by fifty, and quicker in thought and act than we are all the time. The marvel of drugs has always been great to my mind; you can madden a man, calm a man, make him incredibly strong and alert or a helpless log, quicken this passion and allay that, all by means of drugs, and here was a new miracle to be added to this strange armoury of phials the doctors use! But Gibberne was far too eager upon his technical points to enter very keenly into my aspect of the question.

It was the 7th or 8th of August when he told me the distillation that would decide his failure or success for a time was going forward as we talked, and it was on the 10th that he told me the thing was done and the New Accelerator a tangible reality in the world. I met him as I was going up the Sandgate Hill towards Folkestone – I think I was going to get my hair cut; and he came hurrying down to meet me – I suppose he was coming to my house to tell me at once of his success. I remember that his eyes were unusually bright and his face flushed, and I noted even then the swift alacrity of his step.

"It's done," he cried, and gripped my hand, speaking very fast; "it's more than done. Come up to my house and see."

"Really?"

"Really!" he shouted. "Incredibly! Come up and see."

"And it does – twice?"

"It does more, much more. It scares me. Come up and see the stuff. Taste it! Try it! It's the most amazing stuff on earth." He gripped my arm and, walking at such a pace that he forced me into a trot, went shouting with me up the hill. A whole charabancful of people turned and stared at us in unison after the manner of people in charabancs. It was one of those hot, clear days that Folkestone sees so much of, every colour incredibly bright and every outline hard. There was a breeze, of course, but not so much breeze as sufficed under these conditions to keep me cool and dry. I panted for mercy.

"I'm not walking fast, am I?" cried Gibberne, and slackened his pace to a quick march.

"You've been taking some of this stuff," I puffed.

"No," he said. "At the utmost a drop of water that stood in a beaker from which I had washed out the last traces of the stuff. I took some last night, you know. But that is ancient history, now."

"And it goes twice?" I said, nearing his doorway in a grateful perspiration.

"It goes a thousand times, many thousand times!" cried Gibberne, with a dramatic gesture, flinging open his Early English carved oak gate.

"Phew!" said I, and followed him to the door.

"I don't know how many times it goes," he said, with his latch-key in his hand.

"And you—"

"It throws all sorts of light on nervous physiology, it kicks the theory of vision into a perfectly new shape! . . . Heaven knows how many thousand times. We'll try all that after— The thing is to try the stuff now."

"Try the stuff?" I said, as we went along the passage.

"Rather," said Gibberne, turning on me in his study. "There it is in that little green phial there! Unless you happen to be afraid?"

I am a careful man by nature, and only theoretically adventurous. I *was* afraid. But on the other hand there is pride.

"Well," I haggled. "You say you've tried it?"

"I've tried it," he said, "and I don't look hurt by it, do I? I don't even look livery and I *feel*—"

I sat down. "Give me the potion," I said. "If the worst comes to the worst it will save having my hair cut, and that I think is one of the most hateful duties of a civilised man. How do you take the mixture?"

"With water," said Gibberne, whacking down a carafe.

He stood up in front of his desk and regarded me in his easy chair; his manner was suddenly reflected by a touch of the Harley Street specialist. "It's rum stuff, you know," he said.

I made a gesture with my hand.

"I must warn you in the first place as soon as you've got it down to shut your eyes, and open them very cautiously in a minute or so's time. One still sees. The sense of vision is a question of length of vibration, and not of multitude of impacts; but there's a kind of shock to the retina, a nasty giddy confusion just at the time if the eyes are open. Keep 'em shut."

"Shut," I said. "Good!"

"And the next thing is, keep still. Don't begin to whack about. You may fetch something a nasty rap if you do. Remember you will be going several thousand times faster than you ever did before, heart, lungs, muscles, brain – everything – and you will hit hard without knowing it. You won't know it, you know. You'll feel just as you do now. Only everything in the world will seem to be going ever so many thousand times slower than it ever went before. That's what makes it so deuced queer."

"Lor'," I said. "And you mean—"

"You'll see," said he, and took up a measure. He glanced at the material on his desk. "Glasses," he said, "water. All here. Mustn't take too much for the first attempt."

The little phial glucked out its precious contents. "Don't forget what I told you," he said, turning the contents of the measure into a glass in the manner of an Italian waiter measuring whisky. "Sit with the eyes tightly shut and in absolute stillness for two minutes," he said. "Then you will hear me speak."

He added an inch or so of water to the dose in each glass.

"Bye-the-bye," he said, "don't put your glass down. Keep it in your hand and rest your hand on your knee. Yes – so. And now—"

He raised his glass.

"The New Accelerator," I said.

"The New Accelerator," he answered, and we touched glasses and drank, and instantly I closed my eyes.

You know that blank non-existence into which one drops when one has taken "gas." For an indefinite interval it was like that. Then I heard Gibberne telling me to wake up, and I stirred and opened my eyes. There he stood as he had been standing, glass still in hand. It was empty, that was all the difference.

"Well?" said I.

"Nothing out of the way?"

"Nothing. A slight feeling of exhilaration, perhaps. Nothing more."

"Sounds?"

"Things are still," I said. "By Jove! yes! They *are* still. Except the sort of faint pat, patter, like rain falling on different things. What is it?"

"Analysed sounds," I think he said, but I am not sure. He glanced at the window. "Have you ever seen a curtain before a window fixed in that way before?"

I followed his eyes, and there was the end of the curtain, frozen, as it were, corner high, in the act of flapping briskly in the breeze.

"No," said I; "that's odd."

"And here," he said, and opened the hand that held the glass. Naturally I winced, expecting the glass to smash. But so far from smashing it did not even seem to stir; it hung in mid-air – motionless. "Roughly speaking," said Gibberne, "an object in these latitudes falls 16 feet in the first second. This glass is falling 16 feet in a second now. Only, you see, it hasn't been falling yet for the hundredth part of a second. That gives you some idea of the pace of my Accelerator." And he waved his hand round and round, over and over the slowly sinking glass. Finally he tok it by the bottom, pulled it down and placed it very carefully on the table. "Eh?" he said to me, and laughed.

"That seems all right," I said, and began very gingerly to raise myself from my chair. I felt perfectly well, very light and comfortable, and quite confident in my mind. I was going fast all over. My heart, for example, was beating a thousand times a second, but that caused me no discomfort at all. I looked out of the window. An immovable cyclist, head down and with a frozen puff of dust behind his driving-wheel, scorched to overtake a galloping charabanc that did not stir. I gaped in amazement at this incredible spectacle. "Gibberne," I cried, "how long will this confounded stuff last?"

"Heaven knows!" he answered. "Last time I took it I went to bed and slept it off. I tell you, I was frightened. It must have lasted some minutes, I think – it seemed like hours. But after a bit it slows down rather suddenly, I believe."

I was proud to observe that I did not feel frightened – I suppose because there were two of us. "Why shouldn't we go out?" I asked.

"Why not?"

"They'll see us."

"Not they. Goodness, no! Why, we shall be going a thousand times faster than the quickest conjuring trick that was ever done. Come along! Which way shall we go? Window, or door?"

And out by the window we went.

Assuredly of all the strange experiences that I have ever had, or imagined, or read of other people having or imagining, that little raid I made with Gibberne on the Folkestone Leas, under the influence of the New Accelerator, was the strangest and maddest of all. We went out by his gate into the road, and there we made a minute examination of the statuesque passing traffic. The tops of the wheels and some of the legs of the horses of this charabanc, the end of the whip lash and the lower jaw of the conductor – who was just beginning to yawn – were perceptibly in motion, but all the rest of the lumbering conveyance seemed still. And quite noiseless except for a faint rattling that came from one man's throat! And as parts of this frozen edifice there were a driver, you know, and a conductor, and eleven people! The effect as we walked about the thing began by being madly queer and ended by being disagreeable. There they were, people like ourselves and yet not like ourselves, frozen in careless attitudes, caught in mid-gesture. A girl and a man smiled at one another, a leering smile that threatened to last for evermore; a woman in a floppy capelline rested her arm on the rail and stared at Gibberne's house with the unwinking stare of eternity; a man stroked his moustache like a figure of wax, and another stretched a tiresome stiff hand with extended fingers towards his loosened hat. We stared at them, we laughed at them, we made faces at them, and then a sort of disgust of them came upon us, and we turned away and walked round in front of the cyclist towards the Leas.

"Goodness!" cried Gibberne, suddenly; "look there!"

He pointed, and there at the tip of his finger and sliding down the air with wings flapping slowly and at the speed of an exceptionally languid snail – was a bee.

And so we came out upon the Leas. There the thing seemed madder than ever. The band was playing in the upper stand, though all the sound it made for us was a low-pitched, wheezy rattle, a sort of prolonged last sigh that passed at times into a sound like the slow muffled ticking of some monstrous clock. Frozen people stood erect; strange, silent, self-conscious-looking dummies hung unstably in mid-stride, promenading upon the grass. I passed close to a poodle dog suspended in the act of leaping, and watched the slow movement of his legs as he sank to earth. "Lord, look *here!*" cried Gibberne, and we halted for a moment before a magnificent person in white faint-striped flannels, white shoes, and a Panama hat, who turned back to wink at two gaily dressed ladies he had passed. A wink, studied with such leisurely deliberation as we could afford, is an unattractive thing. It loses any quality of alert gaiety, and one remarks that the winking eye does not completely close, that under its drooping lid appears the lower edge of an eyeball and a line of white. "Heaven give me memory," said I, "and I will never wink again."

"Or smile," said Gibberne, with his eye on the lady's answering teeth.

"It's infernally hot, somehow," said I. "Let's go slower."

"Oh, come along!" said Gibberne.

We picked our way among the bath-chairs in the path. Many of the people sitting in the chairs seemed almost natural in their passive poses, but the contorted scarlet of the bandsmen was not a restful thing to see. A purple-faced gentleman was frozen in the midst of a violent struggle to refold his newspaper against the wind; there were many evidences that all these people in their sluggish way were exposed to a considerable breeze, a breeze that had no existence so far as our sensations went. We came out and walked a little way from the crowd, and turned and regarded it. To see all that multitude changed to a picture, smitten rigid, as it were, into the semblance of realistic wax, was impossibly wonderful. It was absurd, of course; but it filled me with an irrational, an exultant sense of superior advantage. Consider the wonder of it! All that I had said and thought and done since the stuff had begun to work in my veins had happened, so far as those people, so far as the world in general went, in the twinkling of an eye. "The New Accelerator—" I began, but Gibberne interrupted me.

"There's that infernal old woman!" he said.

"What old woman?"

"Lives next door to me," said Gibberne. "Has a lapdog that yaps. Gods! The temptation is strong!"

There is something very boyish and impulsive about Gibberne at times. Before I could expostulate with him he had dashed forward, snatched the unfortunate animal out of visible existence, and was running violently with it towards the cliff of the Leas. It was most extraordinary. The little brute, you know, didn't bark or wriggle or make the slightest sign of vitality. It kept quite stiffly in an attitude of somnolent repose, and Gibberne held it by the neck. It was like running about with a dog of wood. "Gibberne," I cried, "put it down!" Then I said something else. "If you run like that, Gibberne," I cried, "you'll set your clothes on fire. Your linen trousers are going brown as it is!"

He clapped his hand on his thigh and stood hesitating on the verge. "Gibberne," I cried, coming up, "put it down. This heat is too much! It's our running so! Two or three miles a second! Friction of the air!"

"What?" he said, glancing at the dog.

"Friction of the air," I shouted. "Friction of the air. Going too fast. Like meteorites and things. Too hot. And, Gibberne! Gibberne! I'm all over pricking and a sort of perspiration. You can see people stirring slightly. I believe the stuff's working off! Put that dog down."

"Eh?" he said.

"It's working off," I repeated. "We're too hot and the stuff's working off! I'm wet through."

He stared at me. Then at the band, the wheezy rattle of whose performance was certainly going faster. Then with a tremendous sweep of the arm he hurled the dog away from him and it went spinning upward, still inanimate, and hung at last over the grouped parasols of a knot of chattering people. Gibberne was gripping my elbow. "By Jove!" he cried. "I believe it is! A sort of hot pricking and – yes. That man's moving his pocket-handkerchief! Perceptibly. We must get out of this sharp."

But we could not get out of it sharply enough. Luckily perhaps! For we might have run, and if we had run we should, I believe, have burst into flames. Almost certainly we should have burst into flames! You know we had neither of us thought of that. . . . But before we could even begin to run the action of the drug had ceased. It was the business of a minute fraction of a second. The effect of the New Accelerator passed like the drawing of a curtain, vanished in the movement of a hand. I heard Gibberne's voice in infinite alarm. "Sit down," he said, and flop, down upon the turf at the edge of the Leas I sat – scorching as I sat. There is a patch of burnt grass there still where I sat down. The whole stagnation seemed to wake up as I did so, the disarticulated vibration of the band rushed together into a blast of music, the promenaders put their feet down and walked their ways, the papers and flags began flapping, smiles passed into words, the winker finished his wink and went on his way complacently, and all the seated people moved and spoke.

The whole world had come alive again, was going as fast as we were, or rather we were going no faster than the rest of the world. It was like slowing down as one comes into a railway station. Everything seemed to spin round for a second or two, I had the most transient feeling of nausea, and that was all. And the little dog which had seemed to hang for a moment when the force of Gibberne's arm was expended fell with a swift acceleration clean through a lady's parasol!

That was the saving of us. Unless it was for one corpulent old gentleman in a bath-chair, who certainly did start at the sight of us and afterwards regarded us at intervals with a darkly suspicious eye, and finally, I believe, said something to his nurse about us, I doubt if a solitary person remarked our sudden appearance among them. Plop! We must have appeared abruptly. We ceased to smoulder almost at once, though the turf beneath me was uncomfortably hot. The attention of everyone – including even the Amusements' Association band, which on this occasion, for the only time in its history, got out of tune – was arrested by the amazing fact, and the still more amazing yapping and uproar caused by the fact, that a respectable, over-fed lapdog sleeping quietly to the east of the bandstand should suddenly fall through the parasol of a lady on the west – in a slightly singed condition due to the extreme velocity of its movements through the air. In these absurd days, too, when we are all trying to be as psychic and silly and superstitious as possible! People got up and trod on other people, chairs were overturned, the Leas policeman ran. How the matter settled itself I do not know – we were much too anxious to disentangle ourselves from the affair and get out of range of the eye of the old gentleman in the bath-chair to make minute inquiries. As soon as we were sufficiently cool and sufficiently recovered from our giddiness and nausea and confusion of mind to do so we stood up and, skirting the crowd, directed our steps back along the road below the Metropole towards Gibberne's house. But amidst the din I heard very distinctly the gentleman who had been sitting beside the lady of the ruptured sunshade using quite unjustifiable threats and language to one of those chair-attendants who have "Inspector" written on their caps. "If you didn't throw the dog," he said, "who *did?*"

The sudden return of movement and familiar noises, and our natural anxiety about ourselves (our clothes were still dreadfully hot, and the fronts of the thighs of Gibberne's white trousers were scorched a drabbish brown), prevented the minute observations I should have liked to make on all these things. Indeed, I really made no observations of any scientific value on that return. The bee, of course, had gone. I looked for that cyclist, but he was already out of sight as we came into the Upper Sandgate Road or hidden from us by traffic; the charabanc, however, with its people now all alive and stirring, was clattering along at a spanking pace almost abreast of the nearer church.

We noted, however, that the window-sill on which we had stepped in getting out of the house was slightly singed, and that the impressions of our feet on the gravel of the path were unusually deep.

So it was I had my first experience of the New Accelerator. Practically we had been running about and saying and doing all sorts of things in the space of a second or so of time. We had lived half an hour while the band had played, perhaps, two bars. But the effect it had upon us was that the whole world had stopped for our convenient inspection. Considering all things, and particularly considering our rashness in venturing out of the house, the experience might certainly have been much more disagreeable than it was. It showed, no doubt, that Gibberne has still much to learn before his preparation is a manageable convenience, but its practicability it certainly demonstrated beyond all cavil.

Since that adventure he has been steadily bringing its use under control, and I have several times, and without the slightest bad result, taken measured doses under his direction;

though I must confess I have not yet ventured abroad again while under its influence. I may mention, for example, that this story has been written at one sitting and without interruption, except for the nibbling of some chocolate, by its means. I began at 6.25, and my watch is now very nearly at the minute past the half-hour. The convenience of securing a long, uninterrupted spell of work in the midst of a day full of engagements cannot be exaggerated. Gibberne is now working at the quantitative handling of his preparation, with especial reference to its distinctive effects upon different types of constitution. He then hopes to find a Retarder with which to dilute its present rather excessive potency. The Retarder will, of course, have the reverse effect to the Accelerator; used alone it should enable the patient to spread a few seconds over many hours of ordinary time, and so to maintain an apathetic inaction, a glacierlike absence of alacrity, amidst the most animated or irritating surroundings. The two things together must necessarily work an entire revolution in civilised existence. It is the beginning of our escape from that Time Garment of which Carlyle speaks. While this Accelerator will enable us to concentrate ourselves with tremendous impact upon any moment or occasion that demands our utmost sense and vigour, the Retarder will enable us to pass in passive tranquillity through infinite hardship and tedium. Perhaps I am a little optimistic about the Retarder, which has indeed still to be discovered, but about the Accelerator there is no possible sort of doubt whatever. Its appearance upon the market in a convenient, controllable, and assimilable form is a matter of the next few months. It will be obtainable of all chemists and druggists, in small green bottles, at a high but, considering its extraordinary qualities, by no means excessive price. Gibberne's Nervous Accelerator it will be called, and he hopes to be able to supply it in three strengths: one in 200, one in 900, and one in 2,000, distinguished by yellow, pink, and white labels respectively.

No doubt its use renders a great number of very extraordinary things possible; for, of course, the most remarkable and, possibly, even criminal proceedings may be effected with impunity by thus dodging, as it were, into the interstices of time. Like all potent preparations it will be liable to abuse. We have, however, discussed this aspect of the question very thoroughly, and we have decided that this is purely a matter of medical jurisprudence and altogether outside our province. We shall manufacture and sell the Accelerator, and, as for the consequences – we shall see.

Trying to Connect You

JOHN ROWE TOWNSEND

Twenty-four hours after I left her, I knew I was wrong and knew what I should have said. I realised clearly, even to the tone of voice, the words that would have made her change her mind and stay in the country; the words that would have brought her on to the canal with me instead of sending her on the night flight to Rome. They were few and simple words, and she was ready to hear them. But they were words unsaid, and perhaps they never would be said. For by now I was floating; was taking my boat along a silent green highway, full of green reflected sky. And with me, instead of Elaine, was amiable, beery old school friend Christopher, happy to oblige at a few hours' notice, easygoing – as a rule – and as comfortable and unexciting as a pair of old shoes.

Twenty-four hours after I left her. A mere four hours before her plane was due to leave Midway Airport. And, growing inside me, the certainty not only that I'd made a disastrous mistake but that I must reach out to her even now, must speak to her, must try at this late stage to put things right. I had a sense of impending catastrophe that went, indeed, beyond reason – a feeling that if she boarded that plane I should never see her again.

A telephone of course was what I needed. But today I'd done all I could to put myself beyond reach of a phone. By now we were in flat, remote and featureless country, far from any road or inhabited place. Without taking my right hand from the tiller, I thumbed left-handed through the canal guide. It was seven miles to the nearest village. There'd be a phone box there, beyond doubt; but there were half a dozen locks in the way, and it took a quarter of an hour to get the *Susie May* through each.

I worked steadily, sweating as I raised and lowered paddles, tempted to cut corners, cursing at each small hitch. The words I should have said to Elaine buzzed remorselessly in my head, in a haze of hope and pain. It began to rain, steadily and coolly beating down on my bare head. I had forgotten to bring my oilskin.

I was working the locks alone by now. Chris, though usually cheerful and easy to get on with, was in a mild state of sulks. He didn't see why we had to press on so hard in these conditions. I'd shown him the village marked on the map, and told him, recklessly, that its pub sold the best beer in the Midlands. But after three locks and what seemed like an inch of rainfall, he wanted to tie up for the night. Further references to the beer produced from him only the remark that we had some on board anyway. In the end he went below and left me to it. It was an uneasy situation, for I knew that by tomorrow he would feel guilty and I a fool. But I went steadily on, not cheered by the thought of the cabin cruiser that had nipped smartly past me and would now be setting all the locks against me. At least I was now so drenched that I could get no wetter.

Light was failing, and the rain had turned to a thick wet penetrating mist, when I came to the last flight of three locks. Beyond it lay a three-mile haul to the village. Yes, there was bound to be a telephone there. But it was after seven o'clock, and if she were to catch the night plane she'd be leaving her flat within half an hour. Half an hour in which to throw the frail line that might hold her, and still three miles to travel. There wasn't a hope. I could make a steady five miles an hour under power, but not until I was through the locks. True, I could tie up and walk along the towpath; but it was dark and muddy, and three miles in half an hour along that gloomy way might as well be thirty. No road, nowhere to beg a lift, nothing but dank sky and flat, anonymous landscape and the rain-pitted surface of the canal. And the only thing that mattered in life, absurdly left undone, was slipping minute by minute out of reach.

I looked round without hope and saw it, improbably perched beside a narrow road that crossed the canal by the next bridge and ran off at a right angle to nowhere. I saw it: a telephone box, all on its own, far from any building, looking as if it might have been sent by Providence for my use. It was the squared pattern of light that I saw, of course, for the framework of the box was visible only in black negative. But there was no mistaking it. It was the one thing I needed, my only hope; and here, in this unpromising stretch of country, it was.

No point in going as far as the bridge. It would be best to tie up at once and cut off a corner on foot. I sounded three sharp pips on the horn, the signal to anyone on board that help was needed. Chris appeared at a hatch, a glass of beer in his hand.

"I'm going to tie up!" I yelled above the sound of the engine.

Chris bawled something back but I couldn't hear him. I headed in for the bank, at the opposite side from the towpath. Chris disappeared. For a minute or two, nothing happened. I looked at my watch for the twentieth time. In twenty minutes now – perhaps less – she would be on her way. No Chris. I switched off the engine, found rope, stake and mallet, leaped ashore and tied up. Chris appeared, stepping carefully, beside me at the last moment, too late to be of use.

"Looks like the back of beyond," he remarked sourly.

"It *is* the back of bloody beyond."

"No better than where *I* wanted to stop an hour ago. And where's the pub you were talking about? I can't see any pub."

"That's in the village," I said, "three miles away. But there's a telephone box here. I must telephone Elaine."

"Can't see a telephone box either," he said grouchily. "And as for Elaine, I thought . . ."

"Never mind what you thought. I'm in a hurry. The phone box is up there somewhere, hidden by the rise of the bank. I'll see you in a few minutes."

"All right, all right," Chris said. "I'm going back to the beer.

Join me when you're ready. If there's any left by then, I must say, you'll be lucky."

But I was scrambling up the bank that edged the canal at this point. At the top I stopped. A few yards away was an empty, doorless barn that I hadn't noticed before. The phone box couldn't be seen. I took my bearings from the bridge and followed with my eyes the fading line of the road. The box was beside the road, I knew. It must be farther along than I thought, and hidden perhaps by a tree.

I struck out in what looked the right direction. I'd not much more than a quarter-hour left now. The ground was damp and marshy. Water came in over my shoes, but it didn't make much difference; my feet were sopping wet already.

Then I was on the road. A real, metalled road, but so flat and wet that you could hardly tell it from the flat wet land around. A road as empty of traffic as the landscape of feature. No sign of habitation within miles. A road from nowhere to nowhere. Fifty yards ahead of me it made, for no obvious reason, a right-angled turn. Arrow signs warned traffic of the corner, and a stretch of white-painted railing lined the outer edge of the curve.

And there it was, visible again, a short walk beyond the bend; the telephone box. It was empty, of course. Who would be using so isolated a box on so wet a night? Who would ever use it? A little passing car traffic, perhaps. No one could reach it before me tonight. Yet I had a curious sense of panic, a feeling that I must hurry to get there before anyone else did.

There was cause for haste anyway. In less than fifteen minutes now she'd be likely to leave her flat. I ran up to the box, my coat hugged close, face wet with rain, feet squelching.

There was a long list of codes on the wall, but no directory. I needed no directory. My fingers dialled the number automatically, the sequence established by long habit.

While I waited for it to ring out, I felt for silver in my trousers pocket. I had plenty of that, anyway. I waited, coin pressed against the slot. No answer. She might have left already, of course; and Sarah, the friend who shared the flat with her, might well be out, or driving her to the airport.

Burr – burr. Burr – burr. My panic rose as it went on ringing. Absurdly, it hadn't occurred to me until now that there might be no reply. That would be the finish of the affair. At this end, a drenched man in a box in some outlandish, unlikely spot. At the other end a telephone ringing and ringing in a city apartment, ringing and ringing to empty air. By the time I saw her again – if I saw her again – all would have changed, and the chance I had today would be gone for ever.

By habit I was counting the ringing tones. Twelve, thirteen, fourteen, fifteen. Nobody would answer now.

But of course I might have misdialled. I hadn't been attending, hadn't even noticed what I was dialling, had simply left it to my fingers. I pressed on the receiver rest, got the dialling tone, and started again, more carefully. A second to wait, a click, another second's wait, another click. And then the ringing tone again. But not quite the same ringing tone.

And at the fourth ring, somebody answered. "Midway Central 3233." The right number, but not Elaine. It sounded like Sarah.

I pressed my money in.

"Hello!" I said. "Sarah?"

The voice just repeated the number. It was Sarah all right.

"Sarah!" I said again.

"Hello!" said the voice, a shade impatiently.

"Hello! Sarah! This is Alan!"

"It's who? I can hardly hear you."

"It's Alan, Alan!"

"It's who?"

"It's ALAN!"

"Oh."

I was bawling into the mouthpiece now.

"Can you hear me now? It's Alan. I want to speak to Elaine."

"You want to speak to Elaine?" I couldn't tell whether she had heard my last sentence or not. She would know I wanted to speak to Elaine. I always wanted to speak to Elaine.

"Yes!" I shouted.

"What?"

"YES!"

"I can still only just hear you." Sarah's voice in my ear was perfectly clear. "Listen, Alan, I don't think Elaine will speak to you. She's leaving in a few minutes' time. She's hurrying to get ready."

"Tell her I *must* speak to her."

"What?"

"Tell her I must speak to her. Tell her I know I was wrong."

"Tell her you know what?"

"Tell her I've just *got* to speak to her."

"Alan, I can hardly hear a word you say. It's a terrible line. Why don't you dial again and see if you can get a better one? In the meantime, I'll tell her it's you."

"All right."

"What?"

"I said ALL RIGHT!" I put down the receiver. In spite of the cold and wet I was sweating. I dialled again, carefully. A second's wait. A click. Another second. Another click. Then silence. The call hadn't connected. I swore, pressed on the receiver rest, and started dialling again.

Then I realised that someone was beating on the glass of the box. There was a woman outside. Heaven knew where *she'd* sprung from. Damn it, she could wait. I went on dialling. A second's silence. A click. Another second. Another click. Then silence again. I swore, more fiercely.

The door of the box opened. I glared. It was a woman of nondescript middle age, dressed in black.

"Please may I use that phone? My call is urgent."

"My call is urgent too," I said.

But her tone of voice was desperate.

"It's life and death!" she said. "You understand? There's been an accident! A car ran into the railings down the road. A doctor's needed. I must ring a doctor!"

There was no arguing with that. I put down the receiver.

"Can I help?" I asked her.

"No, no. Just let me get at the phone!"

I left the box quickly. The woman went in. I looked down the road to the elbow bend where the white railings were. They could just be distinguished in the gloom. No sign of any accident there. It must be farther along.

I watched the woman through the glass. Dialling, waiting, fidgeting. Then her voice raised. I could hear it but I couldn't hear what she was saying. A pause. The voice raised again. Another pause, the woman fidgeting, then turning round, her face agonised.

I turned my back. I couldn't bear to watch. And while this was going on, I reflected – feeling callous, but unable to help it – Elaine might be leaving the flat, going out of my life for ever.

I waited, stamping wet feet. Hell, it must be taking a long time to find a doctor. Was she going about it the right way? Weren't there emergency services? Should I offer to do it for her?

I turned back towards the box again. And the woman had gone.

Strange. Almost incredible. How could she have left the box without my noticing? Wouldn't she have made *some* move to show me that she'd finished? And where had she gone? There was no car nearby, not a soul in sight. I hadn't heard any footsteps.

Anyway, it was nothing to do with me. I must speak to Elaine if I could. I went back into the box, grabbed the receiver, dialled again. And the ringing tone came. Well, come on, Sarah or Elaine, answer it, answer it! *Burr – burr. Burr – burr.* Ten eleven, twelve times. They weren't going to answer.

Well, that was the end. Nothing I could do now.

But . . . I'd misdialled once. Could I have done it again? I pressed on the receiver rest and spelled out the number again, slowly and carefully, making sure.

A second's wait. A click. Another second. Another click. Silence.

I tried once more. A second's wait, a click, another second, another click, silence again.

Oh, the cussedness of things! I dialled for the operator. She answered promptly.

"Number, please."

I told her the number and said I couldn't get it to ring out.

"I'll try it for you. Just hold the line, please."

I held. A long pause. The operator's voice again. No, it wasn't ringing out. There might be a fault. They could have the line tested . . .

"But I spoke to that number a few minutes ago," I said.

"I'll see what I can do. Hold on again, please."

Another long pause. Then the operator's voice once more. "We're getting the engaged signal now."

"*Engaged?*"

"Yes. Shall I keep the call in for you?"

"Yes, please."

"I'll ring you back. What is your number, please?"

I gave it, hung up, and turned to see that there were now two people outside the box. I groaned and opened the door.

"I'm waiting for a call," I said.

The nearer figure was that of a man wearing a black overcoat. His face was pale.

"Let me in, please," he said. "This can't wait. I need to call the fire brigade."

I left the box and he entered it. I spoke to his companion, who stayed outside.

"Where's the fire?" I asked.

"Down near the canal bank. An empty barn. Some kids were playing with matches, burning old hay. When it got out of hand they ran away. But one's missing. He might be still inside."

"How horrible! Can anything be done?"

"I don't think so. Lots people down there now, but they can't get in for the heat and smoke. I think John – that's my friend in the box – will have to call the police and ambulance too. He'll be in there for a few minutes."

"It's a wet night for a big fire," I said.

"Wet?" the man said. His clothes were dry. "Well, I suppose

it *was* wet earlier on. You seem to have been caught in it."

I realised that the rain had stopped, though the air still felt damp. Something was puzzling me, though.

"I only came up from the canal bank a few minutes ago," I said. "I'm surprised I haven't seen or smelled anything."

"Go a hundred yards that way and you'll see it all right," the man said.

His friend John, in the phone box, was still busy. I had almost given up hope now of speaking to Elaine. I walked off in the direction indicated, which was across country towards the canal. But there was still no smell of fire, no flames to be seen. Baffled, I headed back to the box. I'd only been away from it for a couple of minutes. But it was empty. Both men had gone. No car had started, no one was on the road, but they'd gone.

I went in once more, wondering if the operator could have tried in vain to call me back while John was on the line. I waited a minute to see if the phone would ring, but it didn't. So I dialled for the operator. It was a different operator, as you might expect, and she didn't know anything about it. But a brief conference in the exchange brought on to the line the operator I'd spoken to before.

"Oh, yes," she said. "I got the number, but by then your line was engaged. I couldn't hold them, they seemed to be in some kind of hurry. Would you like me to try again?"

"Yes, please."

Delay again. The tension of sheer helpless delay is probably the worst tension of all. My palms were damp. And I was mystified and uneasy. Why all these disasters? What was going on?

Then the operator's voice once more. "I'm sorry, I'm still trying to connect you. We're having difficulty again. Would you like to replace the receiver, and I'll call you when we get through. We have your number."

From the corner of my eye I could see more figures outside the telephone box. This was getting ridiculous.

"No, thank you," I said. "I'll hold on now until you get the call."

I stuck grimly to the receiver. From time to time, deceitfully, I mouthed words as if I were actually speaking to someone. But the number of people outside grew. It looked as if there were five or six of them, and they were all round the box. Finally somebody put his head round the door.

"I'm sorry," he said, "but there's . . ."

"An urgent call?"

"Well, yes. It's about the crashed airliner, the Rome flight earlier tonight. We're relatives of some people who were on board. We've *got* to ring the hospital."

"The Rome flight? From Midway Airport?"

"Yes, haven't you heard? It crashed just after take-off."

"But it hasn't left yet. I know about it. It's the only Rome flight today. A friend of mine will be on it. It doesn't leave till nine."

The man stared. "It *did* leave at nine. Crashed almost at once. Whatever time do you think it is now?"

"Just after eight."

"Are you all right?" He was looking oddly at me. "It's past midnight."

"Listen, this is ridiculous. My watch could be wrong, but not four hours wrong."

"I don't know or care about your watch." The man was impatient now. "But please will you let us use that telephone?"

"All right," I said wearily. I'd stopped trying to make sense of what anybody said. "Operator!"

But the operator didn't answer. Oh, well, there wasn't a doubt that Elaine would have left the flat by now. I hung up and left the box for the third time.

A car stood in the road. These people must all have come in it. They were talking to each other in anxious incomprehensible whispers. I didn't want to speak to them. I hung about on the fringe of the group for a while. But there was no sign that the phone would become free again. And by now there was no point in waiting. The last trace of hope had vanished. I turned to go away.

At that moment the man in the box must have replaced the receiver, though I didn't see it. I was a few yards from the box, and heading away from it, when the bell began to ring. Once, twice, three times. Maybe the operator had got through to Elaine's flat at last. More likely she was merely going to report another failure. But what the hell? I didn't care either way. I kept on walking. Four rings, five rings, six. It was raining again, but I comforted myself once more with the thought that I couldn't get wetter. And there wasn't only beer on the boat, there was surely a drop of something stronger that would warm me up. Seven rings, eight . . .

Somebody was shouting to me.

"Come back!"

Four or five voices took up the shout.

"Come back! Come back!"

Then they were hurrying after me.

"You were waiting for a call to Midway Central?" asked the man I'd spoken to before.

"Yes."

"Well, here it is."

The receiver was off the hook. I picked it up.

"Your call to Midway Central 3233," the operator said. "Will you please put twenty pence in the slot?"

I didn't believe any longer that I was going to speak to Elaine. But I found the money, pushed it in, heard it clink.

"Go ahead, please."

The next voice was hers.

"Elaine!"

"Alan!"

"I never thought I'd get through to you!" I said.

"I vowed I wouldn't speak to you if you did. But the telephone wouldn't give me any rest, ringing and clicking, and going dead every time we picked up the receiver, and then the operator coming on, twice. I thought there must be some disaster."

"There isn't," I said. "I hope."

"Well, you know I've a booking on tonight's flight to Rome. It leaves less than an hour. I ought to be at the airport now."

"Cancel it," I said.

"Why?"

"Well . . . Actually, some madman's just been telling me a wild tale about a crash on take-off, but it doesn't make any sense when take-off isn't for another hour. Anyway, that's not why I want you to cancel the flight. Oh, Elaine, can't you guess why I'm ringing?"

"I'm not sure that I can."

"Listen. You know what I should have said to you yesterday. You know what question I should have asked. If I'd asked it then, what would you have said?"

A pause. Then, in a low voice, "I'd have said yes."

"Take the question as asked," I said.

Another pause. Then, "Take it as answered."

"I'll be round in the morning, I can't get to you tonight. I'm at the back of beyond, without any transport, except the boat, and I wouldn't get far in that."

"That's all right. But come tomorrow. Don't change your mind."

"Don't change yours."

"I won't."

"Neither will I. Ever."

Outside, the people had all gone, and the car as well. I wasn't surprised at that. I didn't even want to think about it. I was full of delight and astonishment that at last I'd got through to Elaine, in every sense of the phrase. And got through, in the end, so simply and directly. And all was well. Surely all was well.

I started back towards the boat. Two or three hundred yards along the road was the sharp bend with the railings. My previous observation had been correct. The railings were intact and there was no sign of anything wrong. There couldn't have been an accident. Not here.

Then I heard a car approaching, saw its headlights. It was

going fast. Too fast. Far too fast. I knew without thinking what I had to do. I sprang into the road. Instantly the driver must have picked me up in his beam. The brakes screamed. I jumped for safety. The car's speed had halved. The driver hooted at me in fury. Then he rounded the bend and accelerated away along the road towards whatever part of nowhere he was heading for. Would he never know he'd been saved from crashing? That was something I'd never know myself.

I left the road and made for the canal bank. As I drew near it I saw the barn. There hadn't been any fire. Nothing of the sort. Out of curiosity I stepped towards the empty, doorless entrance.

There was a rustle of furtive movement. I shone my torch suddenly into a corner, and picked up three small guilty boys in its light.

"What are you doing here?"

"Nothing, mister. Just playing."

I didn't think about what I was going to say. It came automatically to my lips.

"Give me those matches!" I rapped.

"Wh – what matches?"

"You know what I mean. Give me them at once!"

"You've no right, mister . . ." one of them began. But the other was putting a box of matches meekly into my hand.

"Thank you," I said. "Another time, have more sense!"

I walked on towards the boat. It wasn't possible any more to avoid thinking. By the time I arrived, my legs felt curiously weak.

Chris was standing on the canal bank. He greeted me impatiently.

"I've been to look for you once," he said, "and I couldn't find you. Thought you must have fallen into the cut or got run over or something."

"I told you, I went to make a telephone call. And now I've to go back and make another."

He stared at me.

"How," I asked, "would you stop a plane leaving from Midway Airport?"

"Why should you want to do that?"

"Well, suppose you knew a particular flight was heading for disaster?"

"How would you know? Have you seen somebody put a bomb in the loo or something?"

"Chris, I'm serious. Suppose it's a premonition, a genuine premonition, the real thing. How could you get them to take you seriously?"

"You couldn't," Chris said. "Not for a premonition. They'd put you down as a nut case. You might stand a better chance with the bomb-in-the-loo story."

"No," I said. "No, that's not on. I'll have to tell them the truth. It might just have an effect, in some oblique way. Somebody might just check something . . ." I halted in uncertainty. "Anyway, I've got to do what I can. If it doesn't work, I can't help it."

"What the hell are you talking about?" said Chris. And then, "Hey, Alan, you're shaking. Something's happened to upset you. Come on board and have a stiff drink, then you'll feel better."

"I can't," I said. "Not yet. I told you, I must go back and make another phone call."

Chris shook his head.

"I give up," he said. "There are times when the things people do defy all reason, and this is one of them. Go where you like. Though I'd be interested to know where you're making these phone calls *from*. There isn't a telephone box up there at all, is there? I looked."

"Maybe you didn't look hard enough," I said. "Maybe you have to need it desperately if you're to find this one." And I added, without quite knowing where the words came from, "Maybe it's just an emergency service."

"You're out of your tiny mind," said Chris. "You could do with Elaine to get you on the rails again. As for me, I'm going back to the beer."

A Sound of Thunder

RAY BRADBURY

The sign on the wall seemed to quaver under a film of sliding warm water. Eckels felt his eyelids blink over his stare, and the sign burned in this momentary darkness:

TIME SAFARI, INC.
SAFARIS TO ANY YEAR IN THE PAST.
YOU NAME THE ANIMAL.
WE TAKE YOU THERE.
YOU SHOOT IT.

A warm phlegm gathered in Eckels' throat; he swallowed and pushed it down. The muscles around his mouth formed a smile as he put his hand slowly out upon the air, and in that hand waved a cheque for ten thousand dollars to the man behind the desk.

"Does this safari guarantee I come back alive?"

"We guarantee nothing," said the official, "except the dinosaurs." He turned. "This is Mr Travis, your Safari Guide in the Past. He'll tell you what and where to shoot. If he says no shooting, no shooting. If you disobey instructions, there's a stiff penalty of another ten thousand dollars, plus possible government action, on your return."

Eckels glanced across the vast office at a mass and tangle, a snaking and humming of wires and steel boxes, at an aurora that flickered now orange, now silver, now blue. There was a sound like a gigantic bonfire burning all of Time, all the years and all the parchment calendars, all the hours piled high and set aflame.

A touch of the hand and this burning would, on the instant, beautifully reverse itself. Eckels remembered the wording in the advertisements to the letter. Out of chars and ashes, out of dust and coals, like golden salamanders, the old years, the green years, might leap; roses sweeten the air, white hair turn Irish-black, wrinkles vanish; all, everything fly back to seed, flee death, rush down to their beginnings, suns rise in western skies and set in glorious easts, moons eat themselves opposite to the custom, all and everything cupping one in another like Chinese boxes, rabbits in hats, all and everything returning to the fresh death, the seed death, the green death, to the time before the beginning. A touch of a hand might do it, the merest touch of a hand.

"Hell and damn," Eckels breathed, the light of the Machine on his thin face. "A real Time Machine." He shook his head. "Makes you think. If the election had gone badly yesterday, I might be here now running away from the results. Thank God Keith won. He'll make a fine President of the United States."

"Yes," said the man behind the desk. "We're lucky. If Deutscher had gotten in, we'd have the worst kind of dictatorship. There's an anti-everything man for you, a militarist, anti-Christ, anti-human, anti-intellectual. People called us up, you know, joking but not joking. Said if Deutscher became President they wanted to go live in 1492. Of course it's not our business to conduct Escapes, but to form Safaris. Anyway, Keith's President now. All you got to worry about is—"

"Shooting my dinosaur," Eckels finished it for him.

"A *Tyrannosaurus rex*. The Thunder Lizard, the damnedest monster in history. Sign this release. Anything happens to you, we're not responsible. Those dinosaurs are hungry."

Eckels flushed angrily. "Trying to scare me!"

"Frankly, yes. We don't want anyone going who'll panic at the first shot. Six Safari leaders were killed last year, and a dozen hunters. We're here to give you the damnedest thrill a *real* hunter ever asked for. Travelling you back sixty million years to bag the biggest damned game in all Time. Your personal cheque's still there. Tear it up."

Mr Eckels looked at the cheque for a long time. His fingers twitched.

"Good luck," said the man behind the desk. "Mr Travis, he's all yours."

They moved silently across the room, taking their guns with them, toward the Machine, toward the silver metal and the roaring light.

First a day and then a night and then a day and then a night, then it was day-night-day-night-day. A week, a month, a year, a decade! A.D. 2055. A.D. 2019. 1999! 1957! Gone! The Machine roared.

They put on their oxygen helmets and tested the intercoms.

Eckels swayed on the padded seat, his face pale, his jaw stiff. He felt the trembling in his arms and he looked down and found his hands tight on the new rifle. There were four other men in the Machine. Travis, the Safari Leader, his assistant, Lesperance, and two other hunters, Billings and Kramer. They sat looking at each other, and the years blazed around them.

"Can these guns get a dinosaur cold?" Eckels felt his mouth saying.

"If you hit them right," said Travis on the helmet radio. "Some dinosaurs have two brains, one in the head, another far down the spinal column. We stay away from those. That's stretching luck. Put your first two shots into the eyes, if you can, blind them, and go back into the brain."

The Machine howled. Time was a film run backward. Suns fled and ten million moons fled after them. "Good God," said Eckels. "Every hunter that ever lived would envy us today. This makes Africa seem like Illinois."

The Machine slowed; its scream fell to a murmur. The Machine stopped.

The sun stopped in the sky.

The fog that had enveloped the Machine blew away and they were in an old time, a very old time indeed, three hunters and two Safari Heads with their blue metal guns across their knees.

"Christ isn't born yet," said Travis. "Moses has not gone to the mountain to talk with God. The Pyramids are still in the earth, waiting to be cut out and put up. *Remember* that, Alexander, Caesar, Napoleon, Hitler – none of them exists."

The men nodded.

"That" – Mr Travis pointed – "is the jungle of sixty million two thousand and fifty-five years before President Keith."

He indicated a metal path that struck off into green wilderness, over steaming swamp, among giant ferns and palms.

"And that," he said, "is the Path, laid by Time Safari for your use. It floats six inches above the earth. Doesn't touch so much as one grass blade, flower, or tree. It's an antigravity metal. Its purpose is to keep you from touching this world of the past in any way. Stay on the Path. Don't go off it. I repeat. *Don't go off.* For *any* reason! If you fall off, there's a penalty. And don't shoot any animal we don't okay."

"Why?" asked Eckels.

They sat in the ancient wilderness. Far birds' cries blew on a wind, and the smell of tar and an old salt sea, moist grasses, and flowers the colour of blood.

"We don't want to change the Future. We don't belong here in the Past. The government doesn't *like* us here. We have to pay big graft to keep our franchise. A Time Machine is damn finicky business. Not knowing it, we might kill an important animal, a small bird, a roach, a flower even, thus destroying an important link in a growing species."

"That's not clear," said Eckels.

"All right," Travis continued, "say we accidentally kill one mouse here. That means all the future families of this one particular mouse are destroyed, right?"

"Right."

"And all the families of the families of that one mouse! With a stamp of your foot, you annihilate first one, then a dozen, then a thousand, a million, a *billion* possible mice!"

"So they're dead," said Eckels. "So what?"

"So what?" Travis snorted quietly. "Well, what about the foxes that'll need those mice to survive? For want of ten mice, a fox dies. For want of ten foxes, a lion starves. For want of a lion, all manner of insects, vultures, infinite billions of life forms are thrown into chaos and destruction. Eventually it all boils down to this: fifty-nine million years later, a cave man, one of a dozen on the *entire* world, goes hunting-wild boar or sabre-tooth tiger for food. But you, friend, have *stepped* on all the tigers in that region. By stepping on *one* single mouse. So the cave man starves. And the cave man, please note, is not just *any* expendable man, no! He is an *entire future nation.* From his loins would have sprung ten sons. From *their* loins one hundred sons, and thus onward to a civilisation. Destroy this one man, and you destroy a race, a people, an entire history of life. It is comparable to slaying some of Adam's grandchildren. The stomp of your foot, on one mouse, could start an earthquake, the effects of which could shake our earth and destinies down through Time, to their very foundations. With the death of that one cave man, a billion others yet unborn are throttled in the womb. Perhaps Rome never rises on its seven hills. Perhaps Europe is forever a dark forest, and only Asia waxes healthy and teeming. Step on a mouse and you crush the Pyramids. Step on a mouse and you leave your print, like a Grand Canyon, across Eternity. Queen Elizabeth might never be born, Washington might not cross the Delaware, there might never be a United States at all. So be careful. Stay on the Path. *Never* step off!"

"I see," said Eckels. "Then it wouldn't pay for us even to touch the *grass?*"

"Correct. Crushing certain plants could add up infinitesimally. A little error here would multiply in sixty million years, all out of proportion. Of course maybe our theory is wrong. Maybe Time *can't* be changed by us. Or maybe it can be changed only in little subtle ways. A dead mouse here makes an insect imbalance there, a population disproportion later, a bad harvest further on, a depression, mass starvation, and, finally, a change in *social* temperament in far-flung countries.

Something much more subtle, like that. Perhaps only a soft breath, a whisper, a hair, pollen on the air, such a slight, slight change that unless you looked close you wouldn't see it. Who knows? Who really can say he knows? We don't know. We're guessing. But until we do know for certain whether our messing around in Time *can* make a big roar or a little rustle in history, we're being damned careful. This Machine, this Path, your clothing and bodies, were sterilised, as you know, before the journey. We wear these oxygen helmets so we can't introduce our bacteria into an ancient atmosphere."

"How do we know which animals to shoot?"

"They're marked with red paint," said Travis. "Today, before our journey, we sent Lesperance here back with the Machine. He came to this particular era and followed certain animals."

"Studying them?"

"Right," said Lesperance. "I track them through their entire existence, noting which of them lives longest. Very few. How many times they mate. Not often. Life's short. When I find one that's going to die when a tree falls on him, or one that drowns in a tar pit, I note the exact hour, minute, and second. I shoot a paint bomb. It leaves a red patch on his hide. We can't miss it. Then I correlate our arrival in the Past so that we meet the Monster not more than two minutes before he would have died anyway. This way, we kill only animals with no future, that are never going to mate again. You see how *careful* we are?"

"But if you came back this morning in Time," said Eckels eagerly, "you must've bumped into *us*, our Safari! How did it turn out? Was it successful? Did all of us get through – alive?"

Travis and Lesperance gave each other a look.

"That'd be a paradox," said the latter. "Time doesn't permit that sort of mess – a man meeting himself. When such occasions threaten, Time steps aside. Like an aeroplane hitting an air pocket. You felt the Machine jump just before we stopped? That was us passing ourselves on the way back to the

Future. We saw nothing. There's no way of telling *if* this expedition was a success, *if* we got our monster, or whether all of – meaning *you*, Mr Eckels – got out alive."

Eckels smiled palely.

"Cut that," said Travis sharply. "Everyone on his feet!"

They were ready to leave the Machine.

The jungle was high and the jungle was broad and the jungle was the entire world forever and forever. Sounds like music and sounds like flying tents filled the sky, and those were pterodactyls soaring with cavernous grey wings, gigantic bats out of a delirium and a night fever. Eckels, balanced on the narrow Path, aimed his rifle playfully.

"Stop that!" said Travis. "Don't even aim for fun, damn it! If your gun should go off—"

Eckels flushed. "Where's our *Tyrannosaurus?*"

Lesperance checked his wrist watch. "Up ahead. We'll bisect his trail in sixty seconds. Look for the red paint, for Christ's sake. Don't shoot till we give the word. Stay on the Path. *Stay on the Path!*"

They moved forward in the wind of morning.

"Strange," murmured Eckels. "Up ahead, sixty million years, Election Day over. Keith made President. Everyone celebrating. And here we are, a million years lost, and they don't exist. The things we worried about for months, a lifetime, not even born or thought about yet."

"Safety catches off, everyone!" ordered Travis. "You, first shot, Eckels. Second, Billings. Third, Kramer."

"I've hunted tiger, wild boar, buffalo, elephant, but Jesus, this is *it*," said Eckels. "I'm shaking like a kid."

"Ah," said Travis.

Everyone stopped.

Travis raised his hand. "Ahead," he whispered. "In the mist. There he is. There's His Royal Majesty now."

The jungle was wide and full of twitterings, rustlings, murmurs, and sighs.

Suddenly it all ceased, as if someone had shut a door.

Silence.

A sound of thunder.

Out of the mist, one hundred yards away, came *Tyrannosaurus rex.*

"Jesus God," whispered Eckels.

"Sh!"

It came on great oiled, resilient, striding legs. It towered thirty feet above half of the trees, a great evil god, folding its delicate watchmaker's claws close to its oily reptilian chest. Each lower leg was a piston, a thousand pounds of white bone, sunk in thick ropes of muscle, sheathed over in a gleam of pebbled skin like the mail of a terrible warrior. Each thigh was a ton of meat, ivory, and steel mesh. And from the great breathing cage of the upper body those two delicate arms dangled out front, arms with hands which might pick up and examine men like toys, while the snake neck coiled. And the head itself, a ton of sculptured stone, lifted easily upon the sky. Its mouth gaped, exposing a fence of teeth like daggers. Its eyes rolled, ostrich eggs, empty of all expression save hunger. It closed its mouth in a death grin. It ran, its pelvic bones crushing aside trees and bushes, its taloned feet clawing damp earth, leaving prints six inches deep wherever it settled its weight. It ran with a gliding ballet step, far too poised and balanced for its ten tons. It moved into a sunlit arena warily, its beautifully reptile hands feeling the air.

"My God!" Eckels twitched his mouth. "It could reach up and grab the moon."

"Sh!" Travis jerked angrily. "He hasn't seen us yet."

"It can't be killed." Eckels pronounced this verdict quietly, as if there could be no argument. He had weighed the evidence and this was his considered opinion. The rifle in his hands seemed a cap gun. "We were fools to come. This is impossible."

"Shut up!" hissed Travis.

"Nightmare."

"Turn around," commanded Travis. "Walk quietly to the Machine. We'll remit one-half your fee."

"I didn't realise it would be this *big*," said Eckels. "I miscalculated, that's all. And now I want out."

"It sees us!"

"There's the red paint on its chest!"

The Thunder Lizard raised itself. Its armoured flesh glittered like a thousand green coins. The coins, crusted with slime, steamed. In the slime, tiny insects wriggled, so that the entire body seemed to twitch and undulate, even while the monster itself did not move. It exhaled. The stink of raw flesh blew down the wilderness.

"Get me out of here," said Eckels. "It was never like this before. I was always sure I'd come through alive. I had good guides, good safaris, and safety. This time, I figured wrong. I've met my match and admit it. This is too much for me to get hold of."

"Don't run," said Lesperance. "Turn around. Hide in the Machine."

"Yes." Eckels seemed to be numb. He looked at his feet as if trying to make them move. He gave a grunt of helplessness.

"Eckels!"

He took a few steps, blinking, shuffling.

"Not *that* way!"

The Monster, at the first motion, lunged forward with a terrible scream. It covered one hundred yards in four seconds. The rifles jerked up and blazed fire. A windstorm from the beast's mouth engulfed them in the stench of slime and old blood. The Monster roared, teeth glittering with sun.

Eckels, not looking back, walked blindly to the edge of the Path, his gun limp in his arms, stepped off the Path, and walked, not knowing it, in the jungle. His feet sank into green moss. His legs moved him, and he felt alone and remote from the events behind.

The rifles cracked again. Their sound was lost in shriek and lizard thunder. The great lever of the reptile's tail swung up, lashed sideways. Trees exploded in clouds of leaf and branch. The Monster twitched its jeweller's hands down to fondle at the men, to twist them in half, to crush them like berries, to cram them into its teeth and its screaming throat. Its boulder-stone eyes levelled with the men. They saw themselves mirrored. They fired at the metallic eyelids and the blazing black iris.

Like a stone idol, like a mountain avalanche, *Tyrannosaurus* fell. Thundering, it clutched trees, pulled them with it. It wrenched and tore the metal Path. The men flung themselves back and away. The body hit, ten tons of cold flesh and stone. The guns fired. The Monster lashed its armoured tail, twitched its snake jaws, and lay still. A fount of blood spurted from its throat. Somewhere inside, a sac of fluids burst. Sickening gushes drenched the hunters. They stood, red and glistening.

The thunder faded.

The jungle was silent. After the avalanche, a green peace. After the nightmare, morning.

Billings and Kramer sat on the pathway and threw up. Travis and Lesperance stood with smoking rifles, cursing steadily.

In the Time Machine, on his face, Eckels lay shivering. He'd found his way back to the Path, climbed into the Machine.

Travis came walking, glanced at Eckels, took cotton gauze from a metal box, and returned to the others, who were sitting on the Path.

"Clean up."

They wiped the blood from their helmets. They began to curse too. The Monster lay, a hill of solid flesh. Within, you could hear the sighs and murmurs as the furthest chambers of it died, the organs malfunctioning, liquids running a final instant from pocket to sac to spleen, everything shutting off, closing up forever. It was like standing by a wrecked locomotive or a steam shovel at quitting time, all valves being released or levered tight. Bones cracked; the tonnage of its own flesh, off balance, dead weight, snapped the delicate forearms, caught underneath. The meat settled, quivering.

Another cracking sound. Overhead, a gigantic tree branch

broke from its heavy mooring, fell. It crashed upon the dead beast with finality.

"There." Lesperance checked his watch. "Right on time. That's the giant tree that was scheduled to fall and kill this animal originally." He glanced at the two hunters. "You want the trophy picture?"

"What?"

"We can't take a trophy back to the Future. The body has to stay right here where it would have died originally, so the insects, birds, and bacteria can get at it, as they were intended to. Everything in balance. The body stays. But we *can* take a picture of you standing near it."

The two men tried to think, but gave up, shaking their heads.

They let themselves be led along the metal Path. They sank wearily into the Machine cushions. They gazed back at the ruined Monster, the stagnating mound, where already strange reptilian birds and golden insects were busy at the steaming armour.

A sound on the floor of the Time Machine stiffened them. Eckels sat there, shivering.

"I'm sorry," he said at last.

"Get up!" cried Travis.

Eckels got up.

"Go out on that Path alone," said Travis. He had his rifle pointed. "You're not coming back in the Machine. We're leaving you here!"

Lesperance seized Travis' arm. "Wait—"

"Stay out of this!" Travis shook his hand away. "This son of a bitch nearly killed us. But it isn't *that* so much. Hell, no. It's his *shoes!* Look at them! He ran off the Path. My God, that *ruins* us! Christ knows how much we'll forfeit. Tens of thousands of dollars of insurance! We guarantee no one leaves the Path. He left it. Oh, the damn fool! I'll have to report to the government. They might revoke our licence to travel. God knows *what* he's done to Time, to History!"

"Take it easy, all he did was kick up some dirt."

"How do we *know?*" cried Travis. "We don't know anything! It's all a damn mystery! Get out there, Eckels!"

Eckels fumbled his shirt. "I'll pay anything. A hundred thousand dollars!"

Travis glared at Eckels' cheque book and spat. "Go out there. The Monster's next to the Path. Stick your arms up to your elbows in his mouth. Then you can come back with us."

"That's unreasonable!"

"The Monster's dead, you yellow bastard. The bullets! The bullets can't be left behind. They don't belong in the Past; they might change something. Here's my knife. Dig them out!"

The jungle was alive again, full of the old tremorings and bird cries. Eckels turned slowly to regard the primeval garbage dump, that hill of nightmares and terror. After a long time, like a sleepwalker, he shuffled out along the Path.

He returned, shuddering, five minutes later, his arms soaked and red to the elbows. He held out his hands. Each held a number of steel bullets. Then he fell. He lay where he fell, not moving.

"You didn't have to make him do that," said Lesperance.

"Didn't I? It's too early to tell." Travis nudged the still body. "He'll live. Next time he won't go hunting game like this. Okay." He jerked his thumb wearily at Lesperance. "Switch on. Let's go home."

1492. 1776. 1812.

They cleaned their hands and faces. They changed their caking shirts and pants. Eckels was up and around again, not speaking. Travis glared at him for a full ten minutes.

"Don't look at me," cried Eckels. "I haven't done anything."

"Who can tell?"

"Just ran off the Path, that's all, a little mud on my shoes – what do you want me to do – get down and pray?"

"We might need it. I'm warning you, Eckels, I might kill you yet. I've got my gun ready."

"I'm innocent. I've done nothing!"

1999. 2000. 2055.

The Machine stopped.

"Get out," said Travis.

The room was there as they had left it. But not the same as they had left it. The same man sat behind the same desk. But the same man did not quite sit behind the same desk.

Travis looked around swiftly. "Everything okay here?" he snapped.

"Fine. Welcome home!"

Travis did not relax. He seemed to be looking at the very atoms of the air itself, at the way the sun poured through the one high window.

"Okay, Eckels, get out. Don't ever come back."

Eckels could not move.

"You heard me," said Travis. "What're you *staring* at?"

Eckels stood smelling of the air, and there was a thing to the air, a chemical taint so subtle, so slight, that only a faint cry of his subliminal senses warned him it was there. The colours, white, grey blue, orange, in the wall, in the furniture, in the sky beyond the window, were . . . were . . . And there was a *feel.* His flesh twitched. His hands twitched. He stood drinking the oddness with the pores of his body. Somewhere, someone must have been screaming one of those whistles that only a dog can hear. His body screamed silence in return. Beyond this room, beyond this wall, beyond this man who was not quite the same man seated at this desk that was not quite the same desk . . . lay an entire world of streets and people. What sort of world it was now, there was no telling. He could feel them moving there, beyond the walls, almost, like so many chess pieces blown in a dry wind. . . .

But the immediate thing was the sign painted on the office wall, the same sign he had read earlier today on first entering.

Somehow, the sign had changed:

TYME SEFARI INC.

SEFARIS TU ANY YEER EN THE PAST.

YU NAIM THE ANIMALL.

WEE TAEK YOU THAIR.
YU SHOOT ITT.

Eckels felt himself fall into a chair. He fumbled crazily at the thick slime on his boots. He held up a clod of dirt, trembling. "No, it *can't* be. Not a *little* thing like that. No!"

Embedded in the mud, glistening green and gold and black, was a butterfly, very beautiful, and very dead.

"Not a little thing like *that!* Not a butterfly!" cried Eckels.

It fell to the floor, an exquisite thing, a small thing that could upset balances and knock down a line of small dominoes and then big dominoes and then gigantic dominoes, all down the years across Time. Eckels' mind whirled. It *couldn't* change things. Killing one butterfly couldn't be *that* important! Could it?

His face was cold. His mouth trembled, asking: "Who – who won the presidential election yesterday?"

The man behind the desk laughed. "You joking? You know damn well. Deutscher, of course! Who else? Not that damn weakling Keith. We got an iron man now, a man with guts, by God!" The official stopped. "What's wrong?"

Eckels moaned. He dropped to his knees. He scrabbled at the golden butterfly with shaking fingers. "Can't we," he pleaded to the world, to himself, to the officials, to the Machine, "can't we take it *back*, can't we *make* it alive again? Can't we start over? Can't we—"

He did not move. Eyes shut, he waited, shivering. He heard Travis breathe loud in the room; he heard Travis shift his rifle, click the safety catch, and raise the weapon.

There was a sound of thunder.

Deadline

RICHARD MATHESON

There are at least two nights a year a doctor doesn't plan on and those are Christmas Eve and New Year's Eve. On Christmas Eve it was Bobby Dascouli's arm burns. I was salving and swathing them about the time I would have been nestled in an easy chair with Ruth eyeing the technicolour doings of the Christmas tree.

So it came as small surprise that ten minutes after we got to my sister Mary's house for the New Year's Eve party my answering service phoned and told me there was an emergency call downtown.

Ruth smiled at me sadly and shook her head. She kissed me on the cheek. "Poor Bill," she said.

"Poor Bill indeed," I said, putting down my first drink of the evening, two-thirds full. I patted her much evident stomach.

"Don't have that baby till I get back," I told her.

"I'll do my bestest," she said.

I gave hurried goodbyes to everyone and left; turning up the collar of my overcoat and crunching over the snow-packed walk to the Ford, milking the choke and finally getting the engine started; driving downtown with that look of dour reflection I've seen on many a GP's face at many a time.

It was after eleven when my tyre chains rattled on to the dark desertion of East Main Street. I drove three blocks north to the address and parked in front of what had been a refined apartment dwelling when my father was in practice. Now it was a boarding-house, ancient, smelling of decay.

In the vestibule I lined the beam of my pencil flashlight over the mail boxes but couldn't find the name. I rang the landlady's bell and stepped over to the hall door. When the buzzer sounded I pushed it open.

At the end of the hall a door opened and a heavy woman emerged. She wore a black sweater over her wrinkled green dress, striped anklets over her heavy stockings, saddle shoes over the anklets. She had no make-up on; the only colour in her face was a chapped redness in her cheeks. Wisps of steel-grey hair hung across her temples. She picked at them as she trundled down the dim hallway towards me.

"You the doctor?" she asked.

I said I was.

"I'm the one called ya," she said. "There's an old guy up the fourth floor says he's dyin'."

"What room?" I asked.

"I'll show ya."

I followed her wheezing ascent up the stairs. We stopped in front of room 47 and she rapped on the thin panelling of the door, then pushed it open.

"In here," she said.

As I entered I saw him lying on an iron bed. His body had the flaccidity of a discarded doll. At his sides, frail hands lay motionless, topographed with knots of vein, islanded with liver spots. His skin was the brown of old page edges, his face a wasted mask. On the caseless pillow, his head lay still, its white hair straggling across the stripes like threading drifts of snow. There was a pallid stubble on his cheeks. His pale blue eyes were fixed on the ceiling.

As I slipped off my coat I saw that there was no suffering evident. His expression was one of peaceful acceptance as I sat down on the bed and took his wrist. His eyes shifted and he looked at me.

"Hello," I said, smiling.

"Hello," I was surprised by the cognisance of his voice.

The beat of his blood was what I expected, however – a bare trickle of life, a pulsing almost lost beneath the fingers. I put down his hand and laid my palm across his forehead. There was no fever. But then he wasn't sick. He was only running down.

I patted the old man's shoulder and stood, gesturing towards the opposite side of the room. The landlady clumped there with me.

"How long has he been in bed?" I asked.

"Just since this afternoon," she said. "He come down to my room and said he was gonna die tonight."

I stared at her. I'd never come in contact with such a thing. I'd read about it; everyone has. An old man or woman announces that, at a certain time, they'll die and, when the time comes, they do. Who knows what it is; will or prescience or both. All one knows is that it is a strangely awesome thing.

"Has he any relatives?" I asked.

"None I know of," she said.

I nodded.

"Don't understand it," she said.

"What?"

"When he first moved in about a month ago he was all right. Even this afternoon he didn't look sick."

"You never know," I said.

"No. You don't." There was a haunted and uneasy flickering back deep in her eyes.

"Well, there's nothing I can do for him," I said. "He's not in pain. It's just a matter of time."

The landlady nodded.

"How old is he?" I asked.

"He never said."

"I see." I walked back to the bed.

"I heard you," the old man told me.

"Oh?"

"You want to know how old I am."

"How old are you?"

He started to answer, then began coughing drily. I saw a glass of water on the bedside table and, sitting, I propped the old man while he drank a little. Then I put him down again.

"I'm one year old," he said.

It didn't register. I stared down at his calm face. Then, smiling nervously, I put the glass down on the table.

"You don't believe that," he said.

"Well–" I shrugged.

"It's true enough," he said.

I nodded and smiled again.

"I was born on December 31st, 1958," he said. "At midnight."

He closed his eyes. "What's the use?" he said. "I've told a hundred people and none of them understood."

"Tell me about it," I said.

After a few moments, he drew in breath slowly.

"A week after I was born," he said, "I was walking and talking. I was eating by myself. My mother and father couldn't believe their eyes. They took me to a doctor. I don't know what he thought but he didn't do anything. What could he do? I wasn't sick. He sent me home with my mother and father. Precocious growth, he said.

"In another week we were back again. I remember my mother's and father's faces when we drove there. They were afraid of me.

"The doctor didn't know what to do. He called in specialists and they didn't know what to do. I was a normal four-year-old boy. They kept me under observation. They wrote papers about me. I didn't see my father and mother any more."

The old man stopped a moment, then went on in the same mechanical way.

"In another week I was six," he said. "In another week, eight. Nobody understood. They tried everything but there was no answer. And I was ten and twelve. I was fourteen and I ran away because I was sick of being stared at."

He looked at the ceiling for almost a minute.

"You want to hear more?" he asked then.

"Yes," I said, automatically. I was amazed at how easily he spoke.

"In the beginning I tried to fight it," he said. "I went to

doctors and screamed at them. I told them to find out what was wrong with me. But there wasn't anything wrong with me. I was just getting two years older every week.

"Then I got the idea."

I started a little, twitching out of the reverie of staring at him. "Idea?" I asked.

"This is how the story got started," the old man said.

"What story?"

"About the old year and the new year," he said. "The old year is an old man with a beard and a scythe. You know. And the new year is a little baby."

The old man stopped. Down in the street I heard a tyre-screeching car turn a corner and speed past the building.

"I think there have been men like me all through time," the old man said. "Men who live for just a year. I don't know how it happens or why; but, once in a while, it does. That's how the story got started. After a while, people forgot how it started. They think it's a fable now. They think it's symbolic; but it isn't."

The old man turned his worn face towards the wall.

"And I'm 1959," he said, quietly. "That's who I am."

The landlady and I stood in silence looking down at him. Finally, I glanced at her. Abruptly, as if caught in guilt, she turned and hurried across the floor. The door thumped shut behind her.

I looked back at the old man. Suddenly, my breath seemed to stop. I leaned over and picked up his hand. There was no pulse. Shivering, I put down his hand and straightened up. I stood looking down at him. Then, from where I don't know, a chill laced up my back. Without thought, I extended my left hand and the sleeve of my coat slid back across my watch.

To the second.

I drove back to Mary's house unable to get the old man's story out of my mind – or the weary acceptance in his eyes. I kept telling myself it was only a coincidence, but I couldn't quite convince myself.

Mary let me in. The living-room was empty.

"Don't tell me the party's broken up already?" I said.

Mary smiled. "Not broken up," she said. "Just continued at the hospital."

I stared at her, my mind swept blank. Mary took my arm.

"And you'll never guess," she said, "what time Ruth had the sweetest little boy."